Dinner Party   July 22nd.

(8)

Chilled Pink Soup
(buy wholemeal French
    bread Friday)
Lemon Sole stuffed with
Smoked Salmon & Spinach
(check with Jim about fish)
New potatoes, mint
Large green salad

Melon, raspberries or blueberries
        make sorbet
Order cheeses (Friday)

Don't forget to ring Sarah or Emma
to get recipe for corn bread

SEND MAP to Jenny & Chris

Entertaining
WITH
NANETTE NEWMAN
and her daughters SARAH and EMMA

Entertaining
WITH
NANETTE NEWMAN
and her daughters SARAH and EMMA

COLLINS

To the three greatest non-cooks we've ever had the pleasure
of cooking for, Bryan, John and Graham.

First published in 1988 by William Collins Sons & Co. Ltd
London · Glasgow · Sydney · Auckland · Toronto · Johannesburg

1988 Text copyright © Bryan Forbes Limited
Photographs © 1988 William Collins Sons & Co. Ltd

Executive Editor: *Louise Haines*
Cookery Editor: *Carol Bowen*
Design and Art Direction: *Lee Griffiths*
Photography: *Grant Symon*
Stylist: *Gina Carminati*
Home Economist: *Michelle Thomson*

BRITISH LIBRARY CATALOGUING IN PUBLICATION DATA
Entertaining cook book
1. Cookery, International
I. Title
641.5   TX725.A1

ISBN 0 00 412323 9

Typeset by Ace Filmsetting Ltd, Frome, Somerset
Printed and bound in Spain by Cronion S.A., Barcelona

Contents

Useful Facts and Figures

These are just some useful points that we look for when we buy a cookery book:

Metrication

Throughout this book we have given quantities in both metric and Imperial measures. Since exact conversion from Imperial to metric does not usually give practical working quantities, the metric measures have been rounded to the nearest unit of 25 grams. The table below gives the recommended equivalents. However, remember that when making any of the recipes in this book, follow *only* one set of measures as they are not interchangeable.

Ounce	Recommended conversion to nearest unit of 25 grams
1	25
2	50
3	75
4	100
5	150
6	175
7	200
8	225
9	250
10	275
11	300
12	350
13	375
14	400
15	425
16 (1 lb)	450

Liquid Measures

The millilitre has been used in this book and the following table gives a few examples:

Imperial	Recommended millilitre conversion	American cup measure conversion
¼ pint	150 ml	⅔ cup
½ pint	300 ml	1¼ cups
¾ pint	450 ml	scant 2 cups
1 pint	600 ml	2½ cups

Spoon Measures

Spoon measures are level unless otherwise stated.

Egg Sizes

All eggs used refer to size 3 unless otherwise stated. When large eggs are used this refers to sizes 1 or 2.

Quantities

We have suggested how many people each recipe will serve, but naturally, it depends upon your own assessment of your friends' appetites.

Seasonings

Throughout the book we have mainly used fresh herbs but should you use dried, then just remember to halve the quantities.

We are all health-conscious today and many of us wish to cut down on salt, therefore we have not given salt and pepper quantities – this is best left to your own taste and conscience.

Stocks

There is no doubt that home-made stock is by far the best, but don't go into intensive care if you have to use a stock cube. We all do it occasionally.

Fats

Should you prefer to substitute margarine for butter in the recipes they will still work.

Oven Temperatures

Here are the recommended equivalents:

	C	F	gas mark
Very cool	110	225	¼
	120	250	½
Cool	140	275	1
	150	300	2
Moderate	160	325	3
	180	350	4
Moderately hot	190	375	5
	200	400	6
Hot	220	425	7
	230	450	8
Very hot	240	475	9

Foreword

BY NANETTE

I think everyone, if they are honest, has a 'love–hate' attitude to cooking. When it goes well, it's great. When disaster strikes (as it occasionally does with all cooks), it's hateful!

Sometimes cooking every day becomes a chore – it's at times like this that I turn to cook books. Not always for recipes, sometimes just to spark off my imagination or to give me a different version of a well-tried dish. Reading a cook book is to me rather like re-charging the batteries. I think today's cooks have to adjust their culinary talents to many different demands, all within the same household. Cooking leisurely for pleasure, cooking in haste and desperation, cooking for family and friends, or to celebrate a special occasion. There are days when you feel inventive, and there are other days when a sandwich is an effort.

I hope this book will be useful for all those aspects of cooking. Aided and abetted by my daughters, Sarah and Emma, you will be getting three points of view, three attitudes to that one very absorbing subject – for delight and controversy – FOOD!

Nanette on Style

My style of entertaining changes all the time, depending upon the season or which country I'm living in, but the constant factor is the knowledge that it's really the people, not the food, that make the occasion. You could have the greatest gourmet food, in the most sumptuous setting, but if the people are boring – forget it! Scrambled eggs with someone fascinating are infinitely preferable, and more memorable.

I like making the table look pretty and interesting. So many people stick to a bowl of flowers with candles placed either side year in and year out. I think that's dull. I completely change the look of my table all the time. Instead of flowers I might use globe artichokes, or roses in a bowl with mint and rosemary, or masses of tiny vases filled with violets or pansies, or even a huge cabbage with its leaves crammed with white daisies (this looks wonderful for an out-of-doors lunch).

My dining room has a large round table and I prefer to cover it with a tablecloth rather than tablemats. I also love to use odd side plates, bought over the years in junk shops. I don't like large gatherings, unless they're noisy family Sunday lunches. I prefer to invite eight to ten people, and love to build the evening around a celebration, a birthday, an anniversary, welcome home, or Valentine's Day. It's an excuse to use your imagination, and make the people you are entertaining feel special.

I would also rather serve one delicious course and end with fruit and cheese, or a starter and a pudding, than stick to those traditional three courses we all seem obsessed with. I always believe in making your own style, and never copying anyone else's. Create what suits you and your friends best and then enjoy it.

Foreword

BY EMMA

My entertaining can best be described as chaotic. I seem to have a minimum of two dinner parties a week for friends, and although I love every minute of it, I always seem to emerge at the other end wondering how I managed to get everything done.

My sister says she's amazed at my capacity to whip up meals in a flash, and wash and clean up at the same time. This speed is reflected in my style of cooking – I like quick and easy recipes for meals that take the least possible amount of time but look as if I've spent hours slaving over a hot stove.

My mother always wanted us to cook, and instilled in us the courage to experiment, and if it was a disaster, to pretend it was meant to be burnt on top, raw in the middle or to run off the fork.

I enjoy varying recipes – and I also steal recipes from friends (although I hasten to add the ones I *have* stolen for this book have been given full credit).

Emma on Style

My style of entertaining is very informal. I recently got married and we have a small flat where there isn't room to sit many people around a dinner table. So I just lay all the food out, with knives and forks in a jug, a basket of flowers and a basket of fruit, let everyone grab a plate and help themselves. We then sit on cushions around the coffee table. I like my table to be candlelit – the shape, size and colour of the candles, or what they're in, is unimportant – as the effect is lovely. I serve lots of coffee and only invite really close friends. I've never given a business dinner in my life.

Foreword

BY SARAH

I've always been interested in cooking – from mud pies, to a child's obligatory first efforts at chocolate fudge, and cakes that 'never-quite-rose-to-the-occasion' – and I've always been encouraged by my mother to try and do my own thing.

When I left home at seventeen I used to have fantastically ambitious dinner parties. I was never very good at guessing quantities and used to live on leftovers. What I did quickly learn, however, was the ability to make a small event turn into an occasion, by presenting a meal with gusto and making the surroundings pretty and appealing.

I had a few disasters along the way, notably the first time I cooked roast beef for a boyfriend and his entire family. Taking the advice of his mother, I rolled the piece of meat in salt and baked it for over five hours at a very high heat. I can only assume she wasn't crazy about me because the result was not only inedible, but totally ludicrous. This charred, shrunken mass finally smoked its way out of the oven onto a carving board, only to fly like a solid cow pat around the room every time a knife came within a foot of it. I remember sitting in my basement kitchen in London, freezing because all the windows were open to let out the smoke, thinking (as it turned out, accurately) that this relationship was doomed.

I decided from that moment onwards that perhaps there was a grain of truth in the old adage 'the way to a man's heart is through his stomach', and resolved to be less reliant on other people's advice and become more of an instinctive cook.

Now I'm married to the most understanding man in the world, with two babies, I whizz around the kitchen, tripping over toddler trains and soggy teething biscuits, and try to give the illusion of effortless cooking. Undaunted, we have lots of dinner parties – and fun!

Sarah on Style

As everyone in my family knows, I will throw a party to celebrate every conceivable occasion – Christmas, Easter, Hallow'een, Midsummer's Day, birthdays . . . the list is endless. Now that I have two small children my opportunities have increased twofold, and I spend half my life rummaging in kitchen drawers trying to find candles to stick into puddings, since India and Archie are convinced that every time we have anyone over to lunch it warrants a quick, rather breathless, rendition of 'Happy Birthday'.

Because you can nearly always be guaranteed good weather in California, where I currently live, we tend to eat and entertain in the garden. I cover two long tables with French checked tablecloths and use bandanas (the sort cowboys wear around their necks) as napkins. In America you can buy these in any drug store for the equivalent of 50 pence and they come in masses of colours. I stick jars of freshly-picked hibiscus on the table and bottles of opened wine and let everyone sit where they want. I find informality is the only way with small children.

Beginning The Day

Some people couldn't possibly begin the day without breakfast. Others, like me, can only just stagger around, clutching a cup of coffee. That is, until I'm away from home. As soon as I go abroad I become a breakfast addict.

Once when we were living in France, shooting a film, I ate freshly-baked croissants, white peaches and *café au lait* every day – perfection! When we are in America I can't wait to wake up to crispy bacon, easy-over eggs and hash brown potatoes – and I've even succumbed to the odd waffle topped with melted butter and maple syrup. However, as soon as I return home it all becomes a calorie-ridden dream.

I do like getting breakfast for others, on the assumption that, like me, friends staying in my house are 'away-breakfast-eaters'.

The following recipes from Sarah, Emma and me are breakfast ideas that are equally good for brunch, or in some cases, starters, late-night snacks, or simply lovely ways of spoiling friends and family at the beginning of the day.

Nanette

NANETTE

Honeyed Toast

Staying with a friend in Barbados I was given this for breakfast one day. I liked it so much that I had it every morning for the entire holiday.

SERVES 2

2 thick slices granary bread, toasted
2 teaspoons honey
1 banana, thinly sliced
½ mango, peeled, stoned and thinly sliced
2 teaspoons Demerara sugar

Spread the toasted granary bread with the honey. Top with the sliced banana and mango. Sprinkle evenly with the Demerara sugar and cook under a preheated very hot grill until golden and bubbly, about ½ minute.
Serve while still hot.

SARAH

Peanut Butter French Toast

I invented this recipe for my daughter who loves peanut butter but hates breakfast. Since she's only three, she reckons I've lost my mind when she's served this first thing in the morning – but eaten with some fresh sliced fruit it's a great nutritional start to the day.

SERVES 2

4 slices wholewheat or raisin bread
2 tablespoons chunky peanut butter
1 egg
¼ teaspoon salt
4 tablespoons milk
25 g (1 oz) butter

Use the bread and peanut butter to make two sandwiches. Beat the egg with the salt and milk, mixing well. Dip the sandwiches into the egg mixture to coat on all sides.
Melt the butter in a frying pan, add the sandwiches and sauté until golden – about 2 minutes on each side. Drain on absorbent paper.
Serve while still warm cut into thick fingers.

* This recipe is only for people who weigh less than 25 lb or who won't mind putting on 25 lb before the newspaper arrives!

EMMA

Sunday Brunch

These are recipes that I enjoy making and eating late on Sunday mornings. We sometimes have friends in for this breakfast-cum-lunch.

Poor Man's Lox and Bagels

In America lox is used for this recipe – in England we use smoked salmon but this is my economical version.

MAKES 4

4 bagels
8 rashers lean back bacon, rinded
4 tablespoons cream cheese

Split the bagels in half and toast. Grill the bacon until crisp, drain on absorbent paper. Spread one side of each bagel with the cream cheese. Top with the bacon and sandwich together.

Yoghurt with Fruit and Honey

SERVES 4

600 ml (1 pint) Greek-style yoghurt
2–4 tablespoons clear honey
4 tablespoons muesli
2 tablespoons raisins
2 tablespoons flaked almonds
about 225 g (8 oz) of your favourite fruit

Mix the yoghurt with the honey, muesli, raisins and almonds. Spoon into bowls and top with the fruit.

BLTs in Muffins

MAKES 8

8 wholemeal English muffins
8 rashers lean back bacon, rinded
about ¼ shredded Iceberg lettuce
3 tomatoes, thinly sliced
8 teaspoons mayonnaise

Split the muffins in half and toast. Grill the bacon until crisp, drain on absorbent paper. Sandwich the warm toasted muffins with the lettuce, tomatoes, bacon and mayonnaise.

POOR MAN'S LOX AND BAGELS, BLTS IN MUFFINS AND YOGHURT WITH FRUIT AND HONEY

EMMA

High Protein 'Get-Up-and-Go' Milkshake

I'm mad about milkshakes – this one in particular.

SERVES 2

600 ml (1 pint) milk
1 large ripe banana, peeled
1 tablespoon honey
1 teaspoon lecithin granules (available from health food shops)
1 egg
1 teaspoon coffee powder

Place the milk, banana, honey, lecithin granules, egg and coffee powder in a blender or food processor and purée until smooth and creamy. Pour into tall glasses.

NANETTE

Egg-filled Tomatoes

Serve these for breakfast or brunch, or try serving them with Sarah's Cheddar Cheese and Basil Popovers and a crisp salad for lunch.

SERVES 4

4 very large tomatoes
4 rashers streaky bacon, rinded
15 g (½ oz) butter
50 g (2 oz) button mushrooms, wiped and chopped
4 eggs
salt
freshly ground black pepper

Lightly grease an ovenproof dish. Cut the tops off the tomatoes and carefully scoop out the flesh using a teaspoon. Turn the tomato shells upside-down and leave to drain.

Grill the bacon until crisp, drain on absorbent paper then crumble. Melt the butter in a small pan, add the mushrooms and cook until just tender. Mix half of the mushrooms with the bacon and spoon into the tomato shells.

Crack an egg carefully into each tomato, season with salt and pepper to taste then top with the remaining bacon. Place the tomatoes in the ovenproof dish and bake in a preheated oven, 190°C/375°F (gas mark 5), for about 8 minutes, or until the eggs are cooked to your liking.

Variation: Prepare and cook as above but leave out the bacon. Mix all the mushrooms with 3 tablespoons double cream and spoon into the tomato shells. Crack an egg carefully into each tomato, season with salt and pepper and sprinkle with a little grated cheese. Bake as above.

EMMA

'Alternative Breakfast . . .'

Many people detest the sight of breakfast but I really need it to start the day well. I am mad about peanut butter and can eat it anytime – this breakfast idea is dedicated to other peanut lovers.

SERVES 1

2 slices wholemeal bread, toasted
2 tablespoons peanut butter
1 apple, cored and sliced
2 teaspoons clear honey

Spread the toasted wholemeal bread with the peanut butter. Top with the sliced apple and drizzle the honey over.

NANETTE

Energy Non-breakfast

If you can't face food first thing in the morning but have to be on the go all day – try this.

SERVES 1

2 lemon-flavoured Vitamin C tablets
100 ml (4 fl oz) orange juice
1 peach, skinned and stoned
250 ml (8 fl oz) skimmed milk
2 teaspoons clear honey
pinch of ground nutmeg

Dissolve the Vitamin C tablets in the orange juice. Place the peach, milk, honey and nutmeg in a blender or food processor and purée until smooth. Add the orange juice and blend. Pour into a tall glass.

Beginning The Day

SARAH

Celebration Breakfast

Every man I've ever known claims to be able to cook boiled eggs; I plan on teaching my son to make these instead, in the hope that he will find the way to many a woman's heart!

SERVES 2

2 hard-boiled eggs
2 eggs
2 tablespoons double cream
salt
freshly ground black pepper
knob of butter
2 heaped teaspoons caviar (or 'mock caviar')

Taking great care, tap the ends of the boiled eggs and cut around the top edge to remove a small neat slice (or use an egg slicer). Scoop out the egg and use for another dish.

Beat the eggs with the cream and salt and pepper. Melt the butter in a small pan. Add the egg mixture and cook, over a gentle heat, until creamy and scrambled. Quickly spoon into the egg shells and set in an egg cup. Top each with a spoonful of the caviar and serve at once with buttered toast soldiers.

* Mark Birley is probably one of the most stylish men I've ever met. These eggs are served at Mark's Club and are my very favourite thing to eat.

CELEBRATION BREAKFAST

SARAH

Cheddar Cheese and Basil Popovers

I'd never heard of (or tasted) popovers until I came to live in America, and now I'm hooked. These are deliciously light breads that go with everything – fruit salads for breakfast, eggs for brunch or soups and salads for dinner. The basil is optional and can be left out or replaced with your own favourite herb.
In America you can buy special popover tins but deep muffin tins work as well.

MAKES 9

2 eggs
300 ml (½ pint) milk
150 g (5 oz) self-raising flour
¼ teaspoon salt
40 g (1½ oz) butter, melted
2–3 tablespoons finely-chopped fresh basil
75 g (3 oz) Cheddar cheese, grated

Beat the eggs until foamy then gradually add the milk, mixing well. Sift the flour with the salt and beat into the egg mixture until smooth and creamy. Stir in the melted butter and basil.

Half-fill 9 thickly-buttered ramekin dishes or popover tins with the batter. Top with the grated cheese and the remaining batter.

Bake in a preheated oven, 200°C/400°F (gas mark 6), for 15 minutes. Reduce the oven temperature to 180°C/350°F (gas mark 4), and cook for a further 20 minutes, or until well puffed and golden (rather like individual soufflés). Allow to cool slightly before removing from the dishes or tins. Serve hot with lashings of butter.

SARAH

Grits Soufflé

This is a variation on a traditional Southern recipe and even people who think they won't like grits will love this. I often make it when I've got some leftover ham for a light supper dish, but it's also a huge hit at breakfast with lots of warm buttered toast. Grits are not easy to find but worth hunting around for.

SERVES 4

125 g (4½ oz) grits
1.2 litres (2 pints) milk
50 g (2 oz) butter
1 teaspoon sugar
salt
2 eggs, separated

Mix the grits with the milk, butter and sugar in the top of a double boiler, over gently simmering water. Cook, over a moderate heat, stirring until thickened.

Remove from the heat and add salt to taste. Stir in the egg yolks, mixing well. Whisk the egg whites until they stand in stiff peaks. Fold into the grits mixture with a metal spoon. Pour the batter into a 1.75-litre (3-pint) soufflé dish and bake in a preheated oven, 180°C/350°F (gas mark 4), for 30 minutes. Serve at once.

NANETTE

Breakfast Apples

Baked apples are generally served as a dessert but they are just wonderful for breakfast served with vanilla yoghurt.

SERVES 4

4 large cooking apples, cored
75 g (3 oz) dates or dried figs, chopped
4 teaspoons honey
150 ml (¼ pint) apple juice
25 g (1 oz) butter

Make a shallow cut around the waist of each apple to prevent the skins from bursting during cooking. Fill the cavities of the apples with the chopped dates or figs, pressing the filling down firmly. Place in an ovenproof dish which is just large enough to hold the apples snugly. Spoon a teaspoonful of honey over each apple and pour over the apple juice. Dot with the butter.

Bake in a preheated oven, 180°C/350°F (gas mark 4), for about 45 minutes, basting from time to time, until the apples are tender but not fallen – keep an eye on them. Serve warm or cold with vanilla yoghurt.

EMMA: Evening Apples: Prepare and cook as above but stuff the apples with 25 g (1 oz) raisins mixed with 25 g (1 oz) soft brown sugar, 1 tablespoon honey, 1 peeled and chopped banana, ½ teaspoon ground cinnamon and 1 tablespoon brandy. Serve warm with whipped cream.

SARAH AND EMMA

American Marmalade Muffins

We used to be allowed to make muffins when we were very young because they are foolproof. Our mother taught us to make them, and always let us experiment with different ingredients. These are *our* invention.

MAKES 9

100 g (4 oz) plain wholemeal flour
100 g (4 oz) self-raising flour
1 tablespoon baking powder
25 g (1 oz) sultanas
2 tablespoons soft brown sugar
grated rind of 1 orange
2 eggs, beaten
150 ml (¼ pint) milk
50 ml (2 fl oz) sunflower oil
4 tablespoons orange marmalade

Sift the flours and baking powder together in a large mixing bowl, adding any bran left in the sieve. Stir in the sultanas, sugar and orange rind. In another bowl beat the eggs with the milk and sunflower oil. Add the egg mixture and stir lightly until just blended. Do not overbeat.

Half-fill 9 greased muffin tins with the mixture. Top each with a teaspoon of the marmalade, then spoon the remaining muffin mixture over the top. The muffin tins should be about three-quarters full for baking. Bake in a preheated oven, 200°C/400°F (gas mark 6), for 20–25 minutes.

Leave the muffins to cool slightly then turn out and eat while still warm with butter.

NANETTE

The Muffin Mystery

There is some confusion about muffins. In America there is something called an 'English Muffin' – although I've never come across it in England. Actually, I'd always thought an English muffin was really a crumpet.

What we call an American muffin are those 'bun-like' things. In America there are bran muffins, blueberry muffins, raisin muffins, corn muffins; in fact, you name it and they have a muffin made of it.

Confused? Well don't be – just make them and enjoy them, and remember a muffin, is a muffin, is a muffin (unless, of course, it's a crumpet, or a scone, or a bun!).

MAKES 9

275 g (10 oz) plain flour
25 g (1 oz) caster sugar
1 teaspoon baking powder
½ teaspoon salt
1 egg
250 ml (8 fl oz) milk
50 g (2 oz) butter, melted

Sift the flour, sugar, baking powder and salt together in a large bowl. Beat the egg with the milk and butter. Add to the flour mixture and stir lightly until just blended. Do not overmix.

Three-quarters fill 9 greased muffin tins with the mixture. Bake in a preheated oven, 200°C/400°F (gas mark 6), for 20 minutes.

Cool slightly in their tins before turning out. Serve warm with butter and jam.

Variations: To your basic muffin mixture add 100 g (4 oz) of the following and bake, as above, for about 20–25 minutes:

- ☐ fresh blueberries or hulled blackberries
- ☐ chopped dates
- ☐ chopped fresh apricots or peaches
- ☐ chopped apple with a pinch of ground cinnamon
- ☐ chopped pear with the grated rind of 1 small orange
- ☐ half raisin and half chopped nut
- ☐ fresh cranberries

Muffins are doubly delicious if served with tangerine butter. Simply put the juice of 1 tangerine plus the pulp (without seeds) in a blender or food processor with 100 g (4 oz) butter and 2 teaspoons icing sugar. Blend or process until well mixed. Add the finely-grated rind of 1 tangerine and whirl again. Put into a small dish, cover and chill for at least 30 minutes.

Nanette

MUFFINS

NANETTE

Strawberry Omelette

This is a light omelette for a late Sunday summer breakfast. If the weather is behaving itself, serve with iced tea or coffee.

SERVES 2

4 eggs
1 tablespoon caster sugar
1 tablespoon milk
1 tablespoon water
15 g (½ oz) butter
about 100 g (4 oz) strawberries, hulled and sliced
icing sugar to dust
fresh mint sprigs

Beat the eggs with the sugar, milk and water. Melt the butter in a 15-cm (6-inch) omelette pan and swirl around the base to coat. Pour in half of the egg mixture and cook over a moderate heat, moving around with a palette knife or the back of a fork until nearly set.

Add half of the strawberries and continue to cook until the omelette is done to your liking.

Using a palette knife, double the omelette over to sandwich the strawberries. Slide on to a warmed serving plate and dust with a little sifted icing sugar. Repeat with the remaining egg mixture and strawberries to make a second omelette. Serve at once garnished with mint sprigs. Obviously, this is equally delicious with raspberries or sliced peaches, or any other fruit you happen to like.

Beginning The Day

SARAH

Lemon Marmalade and Toast Pudding

This is one of those impressive little numbers that you can easily whip up when you have friends for breakfast.

SERVES 4–6

40 g (1½ oz) butter
8 large slices bread, crusts removed
4 tablespoons lemon marmalade
600 ml (1 pint) milk
4 eggs, beaten

Butter each slice of bread on both sides and sandwich together in pairs with the lemon marmalade. Cut each sandwich into four. Place the bread in the base of a greased 1.5-litre (2½-pint) ovenproof dish.

Heat the milk in a pan until very hot but not boiling. Beat the eggs in a bowl. Pour the milk over the eggs and whisk until well mixed. Pour over the bread and leave to soak for 10–15 minutes.

Bake in a preheated oven, 200°C/400°F (gas mark 6), for 30–40 minutes until golden, well-risen and set. Serve warm with slices of fresh orange and *crème fraiche* if liked.

This is the easiest way I know of making something similar to *crème fraiche* if you can't buy it in the shops. Whip 300 ml (½ pint) double cream until it stands in soft peaks. Add 300 ml (½ pint) soured cream and whisk lightly to blend. Pour into a storage container, cover and leave in a warm place for 24 hours. Chill thoroughly before using. Makes 600 ml (1 pint).

Sarah

Midway

Midway through the day most people think of eating something, even if it's just an apple with a piece of cheese.

However, I think we are too rigidly conditioned to set meal times, often eating from habit rather than hunger – so here are some of our ideas for people who find themselves disinclined to be slaves to convention. These are recipes, from the three of us, for the middle of the day – but also try them for supper, as a first course or a late-night snack. Pigeon-holing food is as boring as pigeon-holing people.

Nanette

SARAH

Chicken Baguettes

These sandwiches are so easy to prepare and yet they seem special. They are perfect for picnics or weekend lunches with iced beer or Pimms.

SERVES 4–6

1 large French loaf
100 g (4 oz) herb-flavoured cream cheese
1 bunch of watercress, trimmed and chopped
225 g (8 oz) cooked chicken, thinly sliced
2 large tomatoes, chopped
1 red onion, peeled and sliced into rings
olive oil
salt
freshly ground black pepper
½ teaspoon dried oregano

Slice the French loaf in half lengthways and spread each side with the cream cheese.

Top one slice of the loaf with the watercress, chicken, tomatoes and onion. Just before serving, drizzle with a little olive oil, season with salt and pepper to taste and sprinkle with the dried oregano. Cover with the second slice of bread and press together gently. Serve cut into thick wedges.

SARAH

American-style Tuna with Apple Sandwiches

MAKES 8

200 g (7 oz) can tuna in brine, drained
2 sticks of celery, chopped
2 dessert apples, cored and chopped
2 hard-boiled eggs, shelled and chopped
1 bunch of watercress, trimmed and chopped
1 bunch of spring onions, trimmed and chopped
2 teaspoons capers
2 tablespoons mayonnaise
salt
freshly ground black pepper
1 large French loaf

Flake the tuna into a bowl. Add the celery, apples, eggs, watercress, spring onions and capers, mixing well. Fold in the mayonnaise with a dash of salt and pepper.

Slice the French loaf in half lengthways. Toast the cut sides under a preheated hot grill. Cut each slice into about 4 pieces. Pile the tuna mixture onto each slice.

SARAH

American Corn Bread

Very American and very useful to serve with soups, salads and desserts.

MAKES ONE 450-G (1-LB) LOAF ·

175 g (6 oz) yellow cornmeal
50 g (2 oz) plain flour
½ teaspoon baking powder
½ teaspoon salt
350 ml (12 fl oz) buttermilk
25 g (1 oz) butter, melted
1 egg, beaten

Mix the cornmeal with the flour, baking powder and salt. Add the buttermilk, butter and egg and beat to a smooth batter. Pour into a well-greased 450-g (1-lb) loaf tin.

Bake in a preheated oven, 200°C/400°F (gas mark 6), for about 20 minutes. Cool on a wire rack.

EMMA

Sunday Brunch Club Sandwiches

These are great sandwiches to eat at about 3 o'clock on a Sunday afternoon when you haven't had the energy to cook a proper Sunday lunch. Here are my favourite ingredients.

SERVES 2

6 slices freshly-made wholemeal toast
100 g (4 oz) Cheddar cheese, sliced
¼ Iceberg lettuce, shredded
6 slices smoked ham
2 tablespoons mayonnaise
2 tomatoes, sliced
1 tablespoon chutney

Top two slices of the toast with the cheese and grill until bubbly and melted.

Arrange lettuce on two slices of toast and add the ham and mayonnaise. Cover with the slices of cheesy toast, sliced tomatoes and chutney. Top with the remaining toast slices and press down gently. Eat while still hot.

SUNDAY BRUNCH CLUB SANDWICHES

EMMA

Dressed Melon

SERVES 4

2 Ogen or Charentais melons
3 kiwi fruit, peeled and sliced
½ cucumber, peeled and chopped
2 red dessert apples, cored and chopped
juice of 1 lemon
2 avocados, halved, stoned and chopped
Dressing:
3 tablespoons sunflower oil
1 tablespoon raspberry vinegar
2 teaspoons honey
1 tablespoon natural yoghurt
salt
freshly ground black pepper

Halve the melons, scoop out and discard the seeds. Using a melon scoop, baller or tea-spoon, scoop out as much flesh as possible from each melon half and place in a bowl. Reserve the melon shells.

Add the kiwi fruit to the melon with the cucumber, apples and lemon juice. Cover and chill.

To make the dressing, beat the sunflower oil with the raspberry vinegar, honey and yoghurt. Season to taste with salt and pepper.

To serve, mix the chopped avocados with the fruit. Spoon over the dressing then fill the melon shells. Serve with warm granary bread.

SARAH

Risotto with Fresh Peas

This is a great 'comfort' food when you've been ill and are on the way to recovery. I also make this dish for my vegetarian friends.

SERVES 4–6

50 g (2 oz) unsalted butter
3 medium shallots, peeled and finely chopped
225 g (8 oz) Italian risotto rice
350 g (12 oz) shelled fresh peas
900 ml (1½ pints) hot chicken or vegetable stock (or canned chicken or vegetable broth)
100 g (4 oz) button mushrooms, wiped and sliced
salt
freshly ground black pepper
3 tablespoons freshly-grated Parmesan cheese

Melt half of the butter in a large shallow pan. Add the shallots and sauté until soft. Stir in the rice, mixing well and cook for 2 minutes but don't let it brown.

Add the peas and 100 ml (4 fl oz) of the stock or broth. Simmer gently until it has been absorbed by the rice. Add the remaining stock, about 100 ml (4 fl oz) at a time, until it has all been absorbed by the rice – stop when the rice is cooked and just tender (don't let it go mushy whatever you do).

Meanwhile, melt the remaining butter in a small pan. Add the mushrooms and cook until lightly browned. Add to the cooked rice with salt and pepper. Stir and gently fold in the Parmesan cheese and serve at once. This is a delicious lunch dish on its own or as an accompaniment to meat.

NANETTE

My Favourite Tomato Omelette

A really excellent omelette is an any time of the day meal. If you're planning to make omelettes for a lot of people, pile different fillings onto a large bread board, for example, mushrooms, onion, tomatoes, herbs, bacon or ham. Have your omelette pan and your filling at the ready, with absorbent paper to quickly wipe the pan clean after cooking each omelette. Let people choose their own filling. This is a good way of feeding a lot of people in the kitchen while having a glass of wine and a chat.

SERVES 1

15 g (½ oz) butter
2 teaspoons olive oil
1 spring onion, trimmed and chopped
1 tomato, skinned and chopped
some chopped fresh basil
salt
freshly ground black pepper
2 eggs
2 teaspoons cold water
a few extra leaves of fresh basil

In a small pan melt half of the butter with the oil. Add the spring onion and cook gently until softened. Add the tomato, mixing well and cook for 2–3 minutes. Add the basil and salt and pepper to taste. Leave on a very low heat while you make the omelette, stirring occasionally.

Beat the eggs with the water and salt and pepper. Melt the remaining butter until hot in a 15-cm (6-inch) frying pan or omelette pan and swirl around until hot. Pour in the eggs and cook over a moderate heat, moving the set mixture from the sides of the pan by tilting and drawing to the middle, allowing the uncooked mixture to run to the sides. Spoon the cooked tomato and herb mixture over half of the omelette. Run a knife around the edge of the omelette and under the base. Using a palette knife, double the omelette over to sandwich the tomato filling. Slide onto a warmed serving plate and sprinkle with a few extra basil leaves. Serve at once.

NANETTE

Beverly Hills Lunch

I first had this in the Polo Lounge at the Beverly Hills Hotel – you feel healthy just looking at it.

SERVES 6 (DEPENDING UPON THE SIZE OF WATERMELON)

1 whole watermelon, sliced into rounds about 2.5 cm (1 inch) thick

2 peaches, stoned and sliced

1 apple, cored and sliced

1 orange, peeled, pith removed and sliced

1 pear, cored and sliced

about 100 g (4 oz) strawberries, hulled

about 100 g (4 oz) raspberries, hulled

about 100 g (4 oz) black grapes, seeded or blueberries, topped and tailed

175 g (6 oz) cottage cheese

fresh mint sprigs

Cut as many slices of watermelon as you have guests. Place each slice onto a dinner plate. Arrange the peaches, apple, orange, pear, strawberries, raspberries, grapes or blue-berries on top in an attractive pattern, like an artist's palette. Add a small scoop of cottage cheese and garnish with mint.

Serve each one with two slices of black rye bread, which have been sandwiched together with cream cheese then cut into thin fingers.

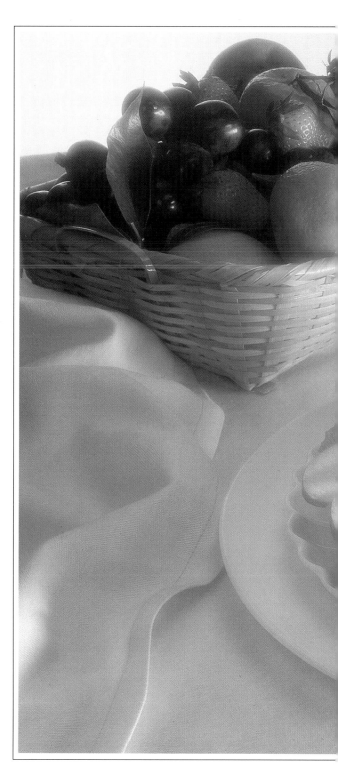

Midway

BEVERLY HILLS LUNCH

Midway

NANETTE

Smoked Gingered Filo Trout

SERVES 4

2 smoked trout, skinned, boned and flaked
juice of 1 lemon
2.5-cm (1-inch) piece root ginger, peeled and grated
1 large tomato, skinned, seeded and cut into strips
3 tablespoons soured cream
2 teaspoons creamed horseradish
1 teaspoon chopped fresh dill
salt
freshly ground black pepper
12 sheets filo pastry
50 g (2 oz) butter, melted

Put the trout in a shallow dish and sprinkle over the lemon juice. Add the ginger and tomato, mixing well. Cover and leave to stand for 15 minutes.

Stir in the soured cream, horseradish, dill and salt and pepper.

Lay out 4 sheets of the filo pastry and brush each with a little of the melted butter. Cover each with another sheet of pastry and brush again with melted butter. Repeat twice to use up all the pastry sheets.

Divide the trout mixture evenly between the pastry piles. Carefully fold into parcels to enclose the filling and brush with any remaining butter. Place each, seam-side down, on a baking tray and bake in a preheated oven, 190°C/375°F (gas mark 5), for 15–20 minutes, until pale brown and crisp.

EMMA

Stuffed Pasta Shells

This is a rich but delicious pasta dish. Serve it with a plain green salad or simple grilled fish.

SERVES 2–3

1 tablespoon olive oil
8–10 large pasta shells
350 g (12 oz) curd cheese
75 g (3 oz) Edam cheese, grated
1 egg, beaten
pinch of ground paprika
salt
freshly ground black pepper
chopped fresh parsley

Bring a large pan of water to the boil and add the olive oil and the pasta. Boil briskly, uncovered, for about 8 minutes (or according to the packet instructions), until the pasta shells are cooked *al dente*. Rinse in cold water and drain thoroughly.

Mix the curd cheese with the Edam cheese, egg, paprika and salt and pepper. Carefully fill the shells with the cheese mixture and place in a buttered ovenproof baking dish. Cover with foil and bake in a preheated oven, 180°C/350°F (gas mark 4), for 15 minutes. Remove the foil and cook for a further 5 minutes.

Serve at once sprinkled with chopped fresh parsley.

NANETTE

Soufflé Pie

This isn't quite a soufflé and it isn't quite a pie – but it is a nice light dish to have with a salad.

SERVES 4–6

a few fresh breadcrumbs
100 g (4 oz) butter
6 eggs, separated
225 g (8 oz) cooked asparagus tips
275 g (10 oz) Cheddar cheese, grated
1 teaspoon salt
1 tablespoon chopped fresh parsley
¼ teaspoon cayenne pepper

Lightly butter and coat a 25- × 15-cm (10- × 6-inch) ovenproof dish with breadcrumbs. Beat the butter and egg yolks in a blender or food processor until pale and fluffy. Stir in the asparagus tips, cheese, salt, parsley and cayenne pepper.

Whisk the egg whites until they stand in stiff peaks. Fold into the cheese mixture. Pour into the prepared dish and bake in a preheated oven, 180°C/350°F (gas mark 4), for 35 minutes, or until puffy and pale brown. Serve at once.

EMMA: Instead of asparagus I use grated carrot. I also vary the cheese and herbs to ring the changes.

SARAH

Spicy Tomato and Arugula Pasta

John spent six weeks working in Italy last year and came back determined to master the art of cooking pasta. It has taken him a long time, a lot of pans, injections of Valium and whisky, but the results are sensational! (For old hats in the kitchen this is a fast sauce!)

SERVES 4 (GENEROUSLY)

4 tablespoons olive oil
3 cloves of garlic, peeled and crushed
½ teaspoon crushed dried red chilli pepper
425 g (15 oz) can Italian plum tomatoes, seeded and puréed
2 teaspoons tomato purée
salt
3 bunches arugula (rocket) or watercress, trimmed
450 g (1 lb) spaghetti or angel-hair pasta
freshly-grated Parmesan cheese to serve

Heat 3 tablespoons of the oil in a large pan. Add the garlic and red chilli pepper and cook for a few minutes. Add the puréed tomatoes, tomato purée and salt, stir thoroughly. Bring to the boil, reduce the heat and simmer gently until the sauce is thickened, about 20 minutes, stirring occasionally.

Bring a large pan of water to the boil and add the remaining olive oil and the pasta. Boil briskly, uncovered, for about 6–8 minutes (or according to the packet instructions), until the pasta is cooked *al dente*. Drain thoroughly.

Place the pasta in a large serving bowl with the arugula (rocket) or watercress and sauce. Toss lightly to mix and serve at once with freshly-grated Parmesan cheese.

Serve with a green salad tossed in a light vinaigrette dressing, if liked.

Arugula (the American name for rocket) is a salad vegetable very popular in Italy, but hardly grown in Britain. It is a small plant with a distinctive flavour. Use watercress instead of the authentic rocket if you are unable to buy it from your specialist greengrocer.

Sarah

SPICY TOMATO AND ARUGULA PASTA

Midway

EMMA

Graham's Hot/Cold Chicken Salad

It is quite a rare occasion when Graham sets foot in the kitchen! However, when he does, he comes out with this dish which I have to admit is wonderful. It is so good that I have nicked it for this book! It was his special batchelor recipe before he married me.

SERVES 4–6

2 tablespoons sunflower oil
6 chicken breasts, skinned, boned and cut into strips
250 ml (8 fl oz) mayonnaise
300 g (10 oz) can waterchestnuts, drained and chopped
4 sticks of celery, chopped
50 g (2 oz) flaked almonds
salt
freshly ground black pepper
juice of 1 lemon
1 family pack of salted crisps
100 g (4 oz) Cheddar cheese, grated

Heat the oil in a frying pan and sauté the chicken until lightly browned. Remove with a slotted spoon and mix with the mayonnaise, waterchestnuts, celery, almonds, salt, pepper and lemon juice. Spoon into a shallow casserole dish.

Lightly crush the crisps and mix with the cheese. Scatter over the chicken mixture, cover with foil and bake in a preheated oven, 180°C/350°F (gas mark 4), for 30–40 minutes until hot and bubbly.

Remove the foil and grill until golden brown. Serve at once with a crisp green salad and interesting bread.

SARAH

Chopped Watercress and Chicken Salad

This is served at the Ivy Restaurant in Beverly Hills. I have copied it unashamedly. It is the perfect salad to sit and munch with a girlfriend – it's quick, easy, nutritious and low in calories. If you want to cheat, serve it with hunks of steaming hot bread!

SERVES 4–6

6 chicken breasts, skinned and boned
chicken stock
6 bunches of watercress, trimmed and chopped very small
Lemon-mustard Vinaigrette:
3 tablespoons fresh lemon juice
3 tablespoons red wine vinegar
250 ml (8 fl oz) olive oil
2 large cloves of garlic, peeled and crushed
1 teaspoon salt
1½ teaspoons Dijon mustard
freshly ground black pepper

Place the chicken breasts in a shallow oven-proof dish with enough chicken stock to just cover. Cover and poach in a preheated oven, 190°C/375°F (gas mark 5), for 15 minutes, or until cooked. Allow to cool completely in the stock.

Remove the chicken from the stock and chop into very small bite-sized pieces. Place in a salad bowl with the watercress and mix.

To make the dressing, place the lemon juice, vinegar, oil, garlic, salt, mustard and pepper to taste in a blender and purée until thick and creamy. Pour over the salad and toss gently.

Midway

EMMA

Bread and Cheese Salad

This salad is a meal in itself. Experiment by adding sliced strawberries.

SERVES 4

225 g (8 oz) cooked ham, thinly sliced and chopped
1 large green dessert apple, cored and chopped
100 g (4 oz) Edam or Emmenthal cheese, rinded and cut into small cubes
½ Iceberg lettuce, shredded
2 tomatoes, sliced
2 heads of chicory, trimmed and chopped
2 tablespoons chopped fresh parsley
a handful of croûtons
Dressing:
3 tablespoons sunflower oil
1 tablespoon wine vinegar
1 teaspoon sugar
½ clove of garlic, peeled and crushed
1 tablespoon wholegrain mustard
pinch of salt

Put the ham in a large salad bowl with the apple, cheese, lettuce, tomatoes, chicory, parsley and croûtons.

To make the dressing, beat the oil with the vinegar, sugar, garlic, mustard and salt. Pour over the salad and toss.

NANETTE

Special Smoked Salad

Followed by fresh fruit and coffee, this makes a delicious light lunch. What could be nicer?

SERVES 4

2 smoked chicken or turkey breasts, skinned and cut into thin strips
1 yellow pepper, cored, seeded and cut into thin strips
6 spring onions, trimmed and cut lengthways into thin strips
2 bunches of watercress, trimmed and finely chopped
225 g (8 oz) small new potatoes, cooked
250 g (8 oz) can lychees, drained
4 tablespoons soured cream
4 tablespoons mayonnaise
1 tablespoon chopped fresh tarragon
salt
freshly ground black pepper
25 g (1 oz) pine nuts, to sprinkle over the top

Mix the chicken or turkey with the pepper, spring onions, watercress, new potatoes and lychees.

Blend the soured cream with the mayonnaise, tarragon and salt and pepper. Fold into the chicken mixture. Spoon the salad onto a large serving plate and sprinkle with pine nuts. Chill.

Midway

NANETTE

Duck and Orange Salad

SERVES 4

4 cooked duck breast fillets, skinned and cut into thin strips
4 oranges, peeled, pith removed and segmented
1 bunch of watercress, trimmed and chopped
1 small radicchio or small bunch of corn salad, trimmed
Dressing:
3 tablespoons sunflower oil
1 tablespoon fresh orange juice
½ teaspoon wholegrain mustard
1 tablespoon chopped fresh chives
salt
freshly ground black pepper

Mix the duck with the oranges and watercress. Arrange on one large or four individual serving plates on a bed of radicchio or corn salad leaves.

To make the dressing, beat the oil with the orange juice, mustard, chives and salt and pepper to taste. Just before serving spoon over the salad.

SARAH

English-style Red Flannel Hash

This is very American and is often eaten for breakfast with an egg on the top, though I prefer it without the egg. It also makes a delicious lunch dish. This is my slightly anglicised version.

SERVES 4–6

50 g (2 oz) butter
1 red onion, peeled and chopped
3 large boiled potatoes, diced
700 g (1½ lb) corned beef, chopped
1 large cooked beetroot, peeled and chopped
150 ml (¼ pint) soured cream
2 tablespoons chopped fresh chives
dash of Worcestershire sauce
2 hard-boiled eggs, shelled and chopped
salt
freshly ground black pepper

Melt the butter in a large heavy-based frying pan. Add the onion and cook until softened, about 5 minutes. Add the potatoes and cook for a few minutes, stirring occasionally.

Add the corned beef and stir, over a low heat, until the mixture is very hot. Add the beetroot and stir around for a minute more.

Meanwhile, mix the soured cream with the chives and Worcestershire sauce. Fold in the hard-boiled egg with salt and pepper. Fold the soured cream mixture into the hot hash. Serve at once.

SARAH   NANETTE   EMMA

Pastry

Everyone has a favourite way of making pastry – here are ours:

SARAH

Savoury Quiche Pastry

MAKES 1 QUANTITY PASTRY (ENOUGH TO LINE A 20- TO 23-CM/8- TO 9-INCH QUICHE)

175 g (6 oz) plain flour
pinch of salt
100 g (4 oz) butter
1 large egg (size 1, 2)
1 tablespoon iced water
2 teaspoons lemon juice

Put the flour, salt and butter in a food processor and process until the mixture resembles fine breadcrumbs. Beat the egg with the water and lemon juice. Add to the dry ingredients with the motor running and process just until the mixture forms a ball. Wrap in clingfilm and chill for 30–40 minutes before using.

Alternatively, if you wish to make it by hand, sift the flour with the salt into a bowl. Rub in the butter until the mixture resembles fine breadcrumbs. Beat the egg with the water and lemon juice. Add to the dry ingredients and mix to a smooth dough. Knead lightly then wrap in clingfilm and chill for 30–40 minutes before using.

NANETTE

Cream Cheese Pastry

MAKES 1 QUANTITY PASTRY (ENOUGH TO LINE A 20- TO 23-CM/8- TO 9-INCH QUICHE)

100 g (4 oz) butter
8 tablespoons cream cheese
150 g (5 oz) plain flour
2 tablespoons sugar (optional)
2 tablespoons double cream

Cream the butter with the cream cheese until fluffy. Sift the flour with the sugar (if used to make a sweet pastry) and stir into the butter mixture with the cream to make a smooth dough. Knead lightly then wrap in clingfilm and chill until ready to use. Use for sweet and savoury flans and tarts.

EMMA

I never bother to make pastry – I buy frozen and just say I've made it. Usually people are very impressed because it's always so good!

SARAH

Tomato and Mozzarella Tart

These quantities are for six people – I usually double the amount since people always want second helpings! You can smell the garlic as you come up the drive.

SERVES 6

Base:

200 g (7 oz) plain flour

175 g (6 oz) butter, chilled

1 tablespoon sugar

salt

3–4 tablespoons iced water

Filling:

3–4 tablespoons Dijon mustard

450 g (1 lb) Mozzarella cheese, thinly sliced

10 large tomatoes, skinned and sliced

1 teaspoon dried oregano

2 tablespoons chopped garlic

freshly ground black pepper

2 tablespoons olive oil

fresh basil leaves

To make the base, sift the flour into a bowl, then rub in the butter until the mixture resembles fine breadcrumbs. Stir in the sugar, a pinch of salt and the water to make a smooth dough. Wrap in clingfilm and chill for 30 minutes.

Roll out the dough on a lightly-floured surface to line a greased 25- × 20-cm (10- × 8-inch) shallow baking tin (this pastry is very fragile and not easy to roll out, don't worry if you have to patch it together).

Spread the mustard over the pastry base and top with the sliced cheese. Cover with the sliced tomatoes, overlapping them slightly. Sprinkle with the oregano, garlic and salt and pepper. Drizzle with the oil and bake in a preheated oven, 200°C/400°F (gas mark 6), for about 40 minutes. Halfway through the cooking time check the pie: if there are excess cooking juices gently spoon away and return the pie to the oven.

Serve hot garnished with fresh basil leaves.

TOMATO AND MOZZARELLA TART

Midway

NANETTE

Uncomplicated Crab Pie

This is the simplest of pies and needs nothing more than a green salad to go with it.

SERVES 4

1 quantity Savoury Quiche Pastry (see page 39)
3 eggs
175 ml (6 fl oz) single cream
1 tablespoon chopped fresh parsley
225 g (8 oz) crabmeat, flaked
salt
freshly ground black pepper
50 g (2 oz) pine nuts

Roll out the pastry on a lightly-floured surface and use to line a 23-cm (9-inch) flan dish or tin. Prick the pastry and bake 'blind' in a preheated oven, 200°C/400°F (gas mark 6), for 10 minutes. Remove and reduce the oven temperature to 180°C/350°F (gas mark 4).

Beat the eggs with the cream, parsley, crabmeat and salt and pepper. Spoon into the pastry case and sprinkle with the pine nuts. Return to the oven and bake for about 40 minutes or until the filling is firm and the pastry is crisp and golden. Serve warm or cold.

EMMA

Gammon and Sweetcorn Quiche

A filling quiche that is perfect for a chilly day. Serve it hot with vegetables or a salad.

SERVES 4–6

370 g (13 oz) packet frozen shortcrust pastry, thawed
75 g (3 oz) cooked gammon, finely chopped
75 g (3 oz) cooked sweetcorn kernels
3 eggs
150 ml (¼ pint) milk
½ teaspoon wholegrain mustard
salt
cayenne pepper

Roll out the pastry and use to line a 20-cm (8-inch) flan tin. Prick the pastry and bake 'blind' in a preheated oven, 190°C/375°F (gas mark 5), for 15 minutes.

Remove from the oven and sprinkle the gammon and sweetcorn over the base. Beat the eggs with the milk, mustard and salt and pepper. Pour into the quiche. Return to the oven and bake for a further 20–25 minutes until the filling is firm.

Serve warm. It is very nice with a cucumber salad.

NANETTE

Parsley Flan

A delicious savoury flan that I serve with a tomato salad. Simply slice ripe tomatoes (skin them if you like – I don't) and drizzle a little oil over them. Season with a few grinds of coarse black pepper, a sprinkling of sea salt and some finely-chopped fresh basil.

SERVES 4

1 quantity Savoury Quiche Pastry (see page 39)
25 g (1 oz) butter
1 onion, peeled and finely chopped
a very large bunch fresh parsley (about the size of a lettuce), finely chopped
3 eggs
150 ml (¼ pint) double cream
salt
freshly ground black pepper
50 g (2 oz) Cheddar cheese, grated

Roll out the pastry and use to line a 23-cm (9-inch) flan dish or tin. Prick the pastry and bake 'blind' in a preheated oven, 200°C/400°F (gas mark 6), for 15 minutes. Remove from the oven and reduce the oven temperature to 180°C/350°F (gas mark 4).

Melt the butter in a pan. Add the onion and cook until softened. Remove from the heat and stir in the parsley. Beat the eggs with the cream and salt and pepper. Add the onion and parsley mixture. Pour into the pastry case and sprinkle with the grated cheese. Return to the oven and bake for about 35 minutes or until the filling is firm. Serve warm or cold.

Weekend Lunches

All three of us find ourselves entertaining quite a bit at weekends. Weekend eating can be given more attention, friends linger, and the meal can happily drift on.

Late Sunday lunch is a good time to gather lots of people together of all ages. So these are some of our recipes for what I suppose you could call 'Proper Lunches'.

Nanette

Weekend Lunches

SARAH

Italian Fish Pie

I've always called this salmon, cod and parsley fish pie 'Italian Fish Pie' because of its colours – red, white and green.

SERVES 4–6

450 g (1 lb) cod fillets
450 ml (¾ pint) milk
salt
freshly ground black pepper
1 bay leaf
50 g (2 oz) butter
3 tablespoons plain flour
2 tablespoons chopped fresh parsley
225 g (8 oz) cooked salmon, flaked
2 hard-boiled eggs, shelled and cut into wedges
about 1 kg (2 lb) mashed potatoes

Poach the cod fillets in the milk with salt, pepper and the bay leaf until tender. Drain, reserving the milk, discarding the bay leaf. Skin and flake the fish.

Melt three-quarters of the butter in a pan. Add the flour and cook for 1 minute. Gradually add the milk, bring to the boil, stirring until smooth and thickened. Season with salt and pepper and stir in the parsley.

Mix the cod with the salmon, eggs and sauce. Spoon into a large shallow ovenproof dish. Top with the mashed potatoes and dot with the remaining butter.

Bake in a preheated oven, 190°C/375°F (gas mark 5), for 30–40 minutes, or until the potato is lightly browned. Serve hot.

NANETTE

Prawns in Lemon Sauce with Tagliatelle

Driving through Italy, we stopped at a tiny, rather tacky, roadside restaurant and were served this delicious dish.

SERVES 4

1 tablespoon olive oil
350 g (12 oz) tagliatelle verdi
300 ml (½ pint) double cream
grated rind of 1 lemon
juice of 1 lemon
salt
freshly ground white pepper
225 g (8 oz) peeled prawns
chopped fresh chervil

Bring a large pan of water to the boil and add the olive oil and the pasta. Boil briskly, uncovered, for about 6 minutes (or according to the packet instructions), until the pasta is cooked *al dente*. Drain thoroughly.

Meanwhile, place the cream, lemon rind, lemon juice and salt and pepper in a pan and bring to the boil. Reduce the heat and cook gently until the sauce thickens. Add the prawns and heat through.

Mix with the pasta and sprinkle with chervil. Serve at once.

NANETTE

Totally Simple Sea Bass

SERVES 4–6

**2.75 g (6 lb) sea bass, cleaned and scaled
fresh fennel or dill sprigs
salt
freshly ground black pepper
juice of 2 lemons
2 tablespoons olive oil**

Using a sharp knife, cut deep diagonal slashes into the flesh of the bass and insert sprigs of fresh fennel or dill. Season the inside of the fish with salt and pepper and stuff with more fresh fennel or dill. Season the outside of the fish with salt and pepper and squeeze over half of the lemon juice and olive oil.

Cook under a preheated hot grill until the flesh is cooked. Turn over carefully and squeeze over the remaining lemon juice and olive oil. Return to the grill and cook until the flesh is tender. Serve hot with any cooking juices poured over the fish and extra chunks of lemon.

Lift simple grilled fish into the luxury class by serving it with this Sorrel Sauce: Remove the hard stems from 1 kg (2 lb) sorrel. Chop finely and cook gently in 40 g (1½ oz) butter until softened, stirring all the time. Add 100 ml (4 fl oz) double cream and salt and pepper to taste. Cook, over a very low heat, for 2–3 minutes until slightly thickened. Stir in 100 ml (4 fl oz) natural yoghurt and cook for ½ minute. Serve warm. Serves 4–6.

Nanette

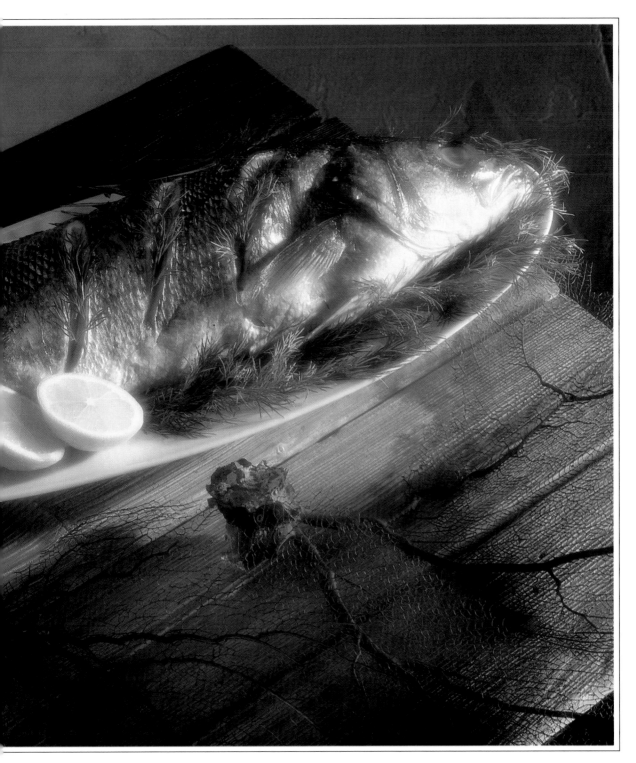

TOTALLY SIMPLE SEA BASS

Weekend Lunches

NANETTE

Smoked Mackerel Gougère

SERVES 4–6

Filling:

25 g (1 oz) butter

1 onion, peeled and chopped

25 g (1 oz) plain flour

150 ml (¼ pint) milk

3 tablespoons dry cider

2 tablespoons natural yoghurt

350 g (12 oz) smoked mackerel, skinned, boned and flaked

3 tablespoons chopped watercress

1 small Cox's apple, peeled, cored and chopped

salt

freshly ground black pepper

Choux Pastry:

300 ml (½ pint) water

50 g (2 oz) butter

175 g (6 oz) plain flour

4 eggs, beaten

75 g (3 oz) Cheddar cheese, grated

1 teaspoon mustard powder

Topping:

1 tablespoon fresh breadcrumbs

25 g (1 oz) flaked almonds

Melt the butter in a pan. Add the onion and sauté until softened and transparent. Stir in the flour, blending well. Gradually add the milk and bring to the boil, stirring all the time. Cook for a further 3 minutes until smooth and thickened, then add the cider, yoghurt, smoked mackerel, watercress, apple and salt and pepper. Remove from the heat and cool.

To make the choux pastry, put the water and butter in a pan and heat until melted then bring to the boil. Remove from the heat, add the flour all at once and beat until smooth. Return to the heat and cook, beating constantly, for about 40 seconds, or until the mixture leaves the sides of the pan clean and forms a ball. Remove from the heat and allow to cool slightly before beating in the eggs, a little at a time, to produce a thick glossy paste. Stir in the cheese, mustard powder and salt and pepper. Spoon the pastry around the edge of a well-buttered 1.75-litre (3-pint) ovenproof dish. Spoon the mackerel filling into the centre and sprinkle with the breadcrumbs and almonds.

Bake in a preheated oven, 200°C/400°F (gas mark 6), for 40–45 minutes, or until the pastry is well-risen and crisp looking. Serve at once.

SARAH: As an alternative, replace the smoked mackerel with smoked trout or smoked chicken.

Weekend Lunches

SARAH

Lobster and Papaya Salad

SERVES 4

2 × 800 g (1¾ lb) boiled fresh lobsters
2 papaya, halved, seeded and finely sliced
2 sticks of celery, chopped
8 canned artichoke hearts, quartered
1 tablespoon brandy
juice of 1 lime
salt
freshly ground black pepper
4 tablespoons mayonnaise
4 tablespoons natural yoghurt
large pinch of cayenne pepper
fresh chervil or dill

Halve the lobsters and remove the flesh. Cut into pieces and place in a bowl with the papaya, celery and artichokes. Mix the brandy with the lime juice and salt and pepper. Pour over the lobster mixture, cover and chill for 30 minutes.

Remove the lobster mixture from the marinade. Mix the mayonnaise with the yoghurt and cayenne pepper. Season with salt and pepper and stir into the lobster mixture. Serve chilled and garnished with fresh chervil or dill.

NANETTE

Coated Red Mullet

SERVES 6

50 g (2 oz) butter
75 g (3 oz) chopped fresh herbs of your choice
6 medium red mullet, cleaned and heads removed
25 g (1 oz) plain flour
250 ml (8 fl oz) dry white wine
juice of 2 lemons

Melt the butter in a large pan. Add the herbs and cook gently for 1 minute. Coat the fish in the flour and add to the pan. Cook gently in the butter mixture for 2 minutes on each side. Press the herbs into the fish skin.

Add the wine and lemon juice and transfer the fish and juice to a shallow ovenproof dish. Cover and bake in a preheated oven, 180°C/350°F (gas mark 4), for 15 minutes.

Remove and place under a preheated hot grill until golden brown and bubbly. Serve at once.

A summer buffet-style lunch or dinner simplifies seating problems. Cover a large table with a wildly pretty sheet. Scoop it up at the corners with bunches of flowers, secured with florist's wire. Make a centrepiece of wild flowers mixed with fragrant herbs.

Nanette

EMMA

Chilled Monkfish with Pears

Leave the garlic out of this dish if you are in love.

SERVES 3–4

450 g (1 lb) monkfish fillets, skinned and cubed
150 ml (¼ pint) water
1 tablespoon lemon juice
salt
freshly ground white pepper
2 dessert pears, peeled, cored and thinly sliced
50 g (2 oz) walnuts
1 bunch of watercress, trimmed and chopped
Dressing:
5 tablespoons olive oil
1 tablespoon white wine vinegar
2 tablespoons chopped fresh tarragon
1 clove of garlic, peeled and crushed
quartered lemon slices

Poach the monkfish in the water and lemon juice with salt and pepper until just tender, about 5 minutes. Drain and cool then chill thoroughly.

If you have time, you can arrange the salad as in the photograph opposite; otherwise, mix the monkfish with the pear slices, walnuts and watercress in a serving bowl or on a large shallow plate.

To make the dressing, blend the oil with the vinegar, tarragon, garlic and salt and pepper to taste. Spoon over the salad and toss gently. Serve with quartered lemon slices.

Weekend Lunches

CHILLED MONKFISH WITH PEARS

NANETTE

Chestnut and Herb Stuffing

This is a nice stuffing for turkey at Christmas – or if you prefer, stuff the turkey with quartered lemons, and bake the stuffing separately in a tin or in muffin tins.

MAKES ENOUGH TO STUFF 1 MEDIUM TO LARGE TURKEY

175 g (6 oz) butter

100 g (4 oz) celery, finely chopped

1 onion, peeled and chopped

1 small green pepper, cored, seeded and chopped

150 g (5 oz) cooked long-grain rice

225 g (8 oz) fresh breadcrumbs

312 g (11 oz) can unsweetened whole chestnuts, drained and crumbled

1 teaspoon dried sage

1 teaspoon dried marjoram

1 teaspoon salt

1 teaspoon ground black pepper

1 tablespoon chopped fresh parsley

2 eggs, beaten

Melt the butter in a pan. Add the celery, onion and green pepper and sauté for 5 minutes until softened.

Add the rice, breadcrumbs, chestnuts, sage, marjoram, salt, pepper and parsley and mix. Bind together with the beaten egg to make a firm stuffing. If the mixture seems a little dry then add a little chicken stock but do not make it too soggy. Cool completely before using.

SARAH

American Corn Bread Stuffing

This delicious corn bread stuffing is a favourite with Americans for their Thanksgiving turkey.

MAKES ENOUGH TO STUFF A MEDIUM TURKEY

100 g (4 oz) celery, finely chopped

1 onion, peeled and chopped

450 ml (¾ pint) chicken stock

about 350–450 g (12–16 oz) corn bread, crumbled (see page 26)

2 eggs, beaten

2 tablespoons chopped fresh parsley

1 tablespoon dried mixed herbs

salt

freshly ground black pepper

Place the celery, onion and chicken stock in a pan. Bring to the boil, lower the heat and simmer until almost tender, about 8 minutes.

Add the corn bread, eggs, parsley, herbs and salt and pepper. Stir well. Cool completely before using.

NANETTE & EMMA

Apricot and Almond Stuffing

Mummy and I did this one Christmas – so we both claim the recipe as our own.

MAKES ENOUGH TO STUFF A LARGE CHICKEN, SMALL TURKEY OR DUCK. DOUBLE THE RECIPE FOR A MEDIUM OR LARGE TURKEY.

15 g (½ oz) butter
1 stick of celery, finely chopped
1 small onion, peeled and chopped
liver from chicken, turkey or duck, chopped
50 g (2 oz) dried apricots, coarsely chopped
50 g (2 oz) flaked almonds
grated rind of 1 lemon
juice of 1 lemon
75 g (3 oz) granary breadcrumbs
salt
freshly ground black pepper
1 egg, beaten

Melt the butter in a pan. Add the celery, onion and chopped liver and sauté for about 5 minutes until softened.

Add the apricots, flaked almonds, lemon rind and juice, breadcrumbs and salt and pepper, mixing well. Bind together with the beaten egg to make a firm but not dry stuffing. Cool before using.

EMMA

Lemon and Apricot Bread Sauce

I often stuff a small turkey with two or three coarsely-chopped lemons and serve it with this sauce.

MAKES 300 ML (½ PINT)

50 g (2 oz) butter
1 onion, peeled and finely chopped
50 g (2 oz) fresh white breadcrumbs
about 4 dried apricots, soaked overnight in cold water and finely chopped
grated rind of ½ lemon
300 ml (½ pint) milk
salt
freshly ground black pepper

Melt the butter in a medium heavy-based pan. Add the onion and cook until softened and translucent.

Add the breadcrumbs, apricots, lemon rind, milk and salt and pepper to taste. Cook, over a low heat, until thick, about 10–15 minutes. Serve hot.

NANETTE

Roast Turkey

Turkey Weight	Oven Temperature	Time
2.5–3.5 kg (6–8 lb)	160°C/325°F (gas mark 3)	2¾–3¼ hours
3.5–4 kg (8–10 lb)	160°C/325°F (gas mark 3)	3¼–3¾ hours
4–6 kg (10–14 lb)	160°C/325°F (gas mark 3)	3¾–4¼ hours
6–8 kg (14–18 lb)	160°C/325°F (gas mark 3)	4¼–4¾ hours
8–10 kg (18–20 lb)	160°C/325°F (gas mark 3)	4¾–5¼ hours

☐ Remember that the turkey, if frozen, must be completely thawed before cooking.

☐ The stuffing must be cold before adding to the bird.

☐ The stuffing must never be added to the bird any longer than the night before cooking.

☐ The turkey should always be kept at a chilled temperature until the time of cooking.

☐ The top of the turkey should be smeared with butter or covered with streaky bacon to prevent drying out.

☐ The whole bird should be wrapped loosely in greased foil for cooking.

☐ The bird should be basted regularly during cooking.

☐ The foil cover should be removed about 45 minutes towards the end of the cooking time to allow browning and crisping.

☐ The turkey should be left to stand, covered with foil, for 15–30 minutes before carving.

SARAH: I cooked the perfect turkey this Christmas by sheer good luck and some good advice – forget how many minutes per pound, try cooking a 6–7 kg (14–16 lb) stuffed turkey for 1 hour breast-side down, 1 hour on the right side, 1 hour on the left side and 20 minutes straight up. Roast at 190°C/375°F (gas mark 5). Use mountains of butter and salt and pepper and above all HAVE FAITH!

EMMA: My contribution to the family dinner was to make the stuffing which was wonderful!

NANETTE: Aren't I lucky to have such modest daughters!

TALKING TURKEY

We still tend to associate turkey with Thanksgiving or Christmas, even though it's an all-the-year-round food. Above are some turkey tips to ensure success. Don't forget a turkey is useful as part of a cold buffet – all the stuffings included in this chapter are equally good hot or cold.

Nanette

NANETTE

Chicken with Apricot and Rice Stuffing

This is simply an interesting version of roast chicken. Serve with steamed young broccoli.

SERVES 4–6

1.6–1.8 kg (3½–4 lb) oven-ready chicken
1 tablespoon sunflower oil
a handful of fresh lemon balm or parsley
2 teaspoons cornflour
juice of 2 oranges
Stuffing:
50 g (2 oz) long-grain rice, cooked
50 g (2 oz) dried apricots, finely chopped
2 sticks of celery, finely chopped
50 g (2 oz) pine nuts, toasted
50 g (2 oz) sultanas
salt
freshly ground black pepper
2 tablespoons natural yoghurt
2 tablespoons chopped fresh tarragon

Rinse the chicken inside and out with cold water then pat dry with absorbent paper.

To make the stuffing, mix the cooked rice with the apricots, celery, pine nuts, sultanas and salt and pepper to taste. Bind together with the yoghurt and tarragon. Spoon the stuffing into the body cavity of the chicken and truss with string to secure.

Put the chicken in a roasting pan and brush with the sunflower oil. Sprinkle with a little salt then cover with the fresh lemon balm or parsley. Roast in a preheated oven, 190°C/375°F (gas mark 5), for 1¼–1½ hours, basting frequently with the pan juices, until the chicken is cooked and the juices run clear. Remove from the oven and transfer to a warmed serving plate. Keep warm.

Dissolve the cornflour in the orange juice and stir into the pan juices. Bring to the boil, stirring until smooth and thickened. If the sauce seems too thick at this stage, then add 2 tablespoons water to thin. Serve with any green vegetable.

SARAH: In the summer try cooking a plain roast chicken and serving it hot with a cold, very minty, vinaigrette dressing – very interesting, very delicious and very easy.

SARAH

Stuffed Boned Chicken

I prefer boned chicken because it's so easy to carve. I also like this stuffing because it's typically English.

SERVES 6

1.6–1.8 kg (3½–4 lb) oven-ready chicken, boned
150 ml (¼ pint) stock
6–8 slices white or wholemeal bread
100 g (4 oz) butter
1 onion, peeled and chopped
½ × 312 g (11 oz) can unsweetened whole chestnuts, drained and chopped
1 tablespoon chopped fresh tarragon
1 tablespoon chopped fresh parsley
1 egg, beaten
sea salt
freshly ground black pepper
1 tablespoon sunflower oil
fresh parsley sprigs

Place the chicken, skin-side down, on a large board. Turn the legs and the wings of the chicken inside out. Pour the stock over the bread and leave to soak.

Melt the butter in a pan. Add the onion and sauté until softened. Remove from the heat and mix in the soaked bread, chestnuts, tarragon, parsley, egg and salt and pepper.

Spread the stuffing mixture over the chicken, draw the sides of the bird together and sew up (using a trussing needle and fine thread) to a good shape. Place in a roasting pan and brush with the sunflower oil. Season with salt and pepper. Roast in a preheated oven, 190°C/375°F (gas mark 5), for about 1¾ hours, until the chicken is cooked.

Remove the thread. Serve hot or cold with vegetables (for example, French beans and carrots) or a salad. Garnish with fresh parsley sprigs.

If you don't have enough space at your table to seat small children with the grown-ups, simply paint each child's name on miniature paper carrier bags, fill with picnic-style food, put out a low coffee table for them to sit at, and they will think it's great fun!

Sarah

STUFFED BONED CHICKEN

NANETTE

Spiced Marinated Lamb

It is said that the way to a man's heart is through his stomach. I have never believed that. However, I do know a woman who says she fell in love with her husband because he was a superb cook. She has never, to my knowledge, set foot in her kitchen other than to make a cup of tea or coffee. After ten years she is still happily married, well fed, and a lot of her women friends can't help turning green occasionally. This was (according to him) the first thing he cooked for her.

SERVES 10–12

2.75 kg (6 lb) leg of lamb
Marinade:
6 large cloves of garlic, peeled
about a 5-cm (2-inch) piece root ginger, peeled
2 teaspoons sea salt
grated rind and juice of 1 large lemon
1 heaped teaspoon cumin powder
½ heaped teaspoon ground turmeric
1 heaped teaspoon dried rosemary
½ heaped teaspoon dried cloves
600 ml (1 pint) natural yoghurt
1½ tablespoons honey

Using a skewer make small holes all over the surface of the lamb deep into the flesh.

Put the garlic, ginger, salt, lemon rind and juice, cumin powder, turmeric, rosemary and cloves in a blender or food processor and purée until smooth. Rub this mixture over the surface of the lamb and place in a roasting pan. Without washing the blender or food processor, add half of the yoghurt and the honey. Whirl around then pour over the lamb. Cover with foil and refrigerate overnight.

To cook the lamb, place in a preheated oven, 220°C/425°F (gas mark 7), for 30 min-

utes. Reduce the oven temperature to 160°C/325°F (gas mark 3), and cook for a further 1½ hours, basting occasionally with the marinade juices. Remove the foil cover and cook for a further 30 minutes. Remove the meat from the pan and place on a warmed serving dish. Keep warm.

Stir the remaining yoghurt into the pan juices and stir briskly over a low heat to blend. Serve hot with the lamb.

* This is obviously not a recipe for those who like their lamb pink and underdone.

NANETTE

Old English Spiced Beef

Clare says this is a godsend at Christmas – she serves it with red cabbage. Saltpetre can be bought from good chemists or from your local butcher's.

SERVES 12

½ teaspoon ground cloves
½ teaspoon ground mace
½ teaspoon coarsely-crushed black peppercorns
½ teaspoon ground allspice
1 tablespoon dried thyme
225 g (8 oz) dark brown sugar
2.25–2.75 kg (5–6 lb) joint brisket or topside of beef
225 g (8 oz) sea salt
15 g (½ oz) saltpetre
6 bay leaves
12 juniper berries, crushed
1 bouquet garni
2 carrots, peeled and chopped
2 sticks of celery, chopped
1 onion, peeled and chopped
200 ml (7 fl oz) port
600 ml (1 pint) beef stock

Mix the cloves with the mace, peppercorns, allspice and thyme. Stir half of this mixture into the sugar and use to cover the unrolled joint of beef. Place in a shallow earthenware dish, cover and leave to stand for 24 hours.

The next day, rub the salt, saltpetre, bay leaves and juniper berries into the beef. Cover and leave to marinate in a cool place for 1 week, rubbing the spices into the meat flesh and turning the joint over daily.

Rinse and soak the joint in cold water for 1 hour. Dry thoroughly on absorbent paper and spread the reserved spices over the meat. Roll up tightly and secure with string.

Place the meat in a large casserole and surround with the bouquet garni, carrots, celery, onion, port and stock. Cover and cook in a preheated oven, 150°C/300°F (gas mark 2), for 4–5 hours, or until very tender. Let it cool in the juices.

Remove the meat and place between two wooden chopping boards with a 450-g (1-lb) weight on top. Leave to stand in a cool place for 12 hours before slicing thinly to serve.

SARAH

Lamb with Rosemary and Garlic

None of my family is a red meat eater but a lot of my friends are – so I sometimes cook this for them. With roast potatoes, new peas and mint sauce it reminds me of English Sunday lunches and Americans love it.

SERVES 6–8

3 cloves of garlic
1.8 kg (4 lb) leg of lamb
2 tablespoons olive oil
2 teaspoons chopped fresh rosemary
½ teaspoon chopped fresh thyme
salt
freshly ground black pepper
150 ml (¼ pint) light stock
juice of 1 lemon
25 g (1 oz) butter

Peel the garlic and cut into thin slivers. Using a sharp, pointed knife or skewer, make small cuts into the lamb and insert a sliver of garlic in each. Place in a roasting pan.

Mix the olive oil with the rosemary, thyme and salt and pepper and pour over the lamb. Roast in a preheated oven, 220°C/425°F (gas mark 7), for 15 minutes. Reduce the oven temperature to 190°C/375°F (gas mark 5), and cook for a further 1¼–1¾ hours, or until the lamb is cooked but still pink towards the centre of the leg – the juices that flow from the lamb when pierced should just be colourless.

Remove the meat from the roasting pan and place on a warmed serving dish. Keep warm. Add the stock to the pan, scraping all the bits. Bring to the boil and add the lemon juice and salt and pepper. Stir in the butter, cut into small pieces, blending well to make a sauce.

Serve cut into slices with a little of the sauce. This is delicious served with a selection of vegetable purées (for example, carrots cooked and puréed with a little potato; parsnips cooked, puréed and seasoned with a little nutmeg and cream; and broccoli cooked and puréed with a little cottage cheese).

LAMB WITH ROSEMARY AND GARLIC

Stay For Tea

If one could ever say that certain meals have gone out of fashion, I suppose tea has. There are still some people who, at four o'clock, continue the time-honoured ritual, but for most of us it is probably more likely to be a tea-bag in the kitchen with a packet of biscuits.

It is, however, occasionally nice to pay a bit more attention to this very English tradition. So conjure up thoughts of tea on a sun-drenched lawn, or in front of a log fire on a winter's afternoon – little sandwiches, scones, spice-scented cake. Ah well, it's pleasant to think about.

Nanette

EMMA

Banana Bread with Grapefruit Cheese Topping

This is a teabread that is marvellous served warm with butter and honey, or cold with a frosted Grapefruit Cream Cheese Topping.

MAKES ONE 450-G (1-LB) LOAF

100 g (4 oz) butter
225 g (8 oz) soft brown sugar
grated rind of 1 small grapefruit
1 egg
2 ripe bananas, peeled and mashed
100 g (4 oz) self-raising flour
100 g (4 oz) plain wholewheat flour
1½ teaspoons baking powder
4 tablespoons natural yoghurt
Grapefruit Cream Cheese Topping:
225 g (8 oz) cream cheese
grated rind of 1 grapefruit
2 tablespoons grapefruit juice
75 g (3 oz) icing sugar, sifted

Cream the butter with the sugar and grapefruit rind until very pale and creamy. Beat in the egg and the mashed bananas.

Sift the flours with the baking powder, adding any bran left in the sieve. Fold into the banana mixture with the yoghurt. Mix very well. Spoon into a greased 450-g (1-lb) loaf tin and level the surface. Bake in a preheated oven, 180°C/350°F (gas mark 4), for 1 hour, or until a skewer inserted comes out clean. Leave to get cold.

To make the topping, beat the cream cheese with the grapefruit rind, grapefruit juice and icing sugar to make a smooth icing. Swirl over the top of the banana loaf.

NANETTE

Prune Cake

MAKES ONE 900-G (2-LB) LOAF

175 g (6 oz) prunes, chopped
225 g (8 oz) plain flour
2 teaspoons baking powder
1 teaspoon ground mixed spice
75 g (3 oz) butter
75 ml (3 fl oz) maple syrup
75 g (3 oz) medium-cut orange marmalade
100 g (4 oz) Demerara sugar
150 ml (¼ pint) milk
1 egg, beaten
50 g (2 oz) chopped apple
50 g (2 oz) broken walnuts
1 tablespoon brown rum

Cook the prunes in a little water until soft. Cool then chop. Sift the flour with the baking powder and mixed spice.

Melt the butter in a large pan with the maple syrup, marmalade and sugar. Add the flour mixture, milk and egg and mix. Stir in the prunes, apple and walnuts.

Spoon into a greased 900-g (2-lb) loaf tin. Bake in a preheated oven, 180°C/350°F (gas mark 4), for 1–1¼ hours, or until a skewer inserted comes out clean. Remove from the tin while still warm. Poke holes using a skewer in the base of the cake and pour over the rum. Leave to cool.

> If you can't ice a cake for a special occasion, you can still make it look wonderful. Join together three or four helium-filled balloons halfway down their strings, then attach the string to a small wooden skewer and plunge into the cake. Add an extravagant ribbon. You'll be surprised how impressed everyone will be.
> *Emma*

SARAH

Foot-high Fudge Cake

In America everything seems to be bigger – not always better but bigger. This four-layer chocolate cake is literally a foot high!

MAKES ONE 23- TO 25-CM (9- TO 10-INCH) CAKE (CUTS INTO 14-16 SLICES)

200 g (7 oz) plain dessert chocolate
150 ml (¼ pint) milk
150 ml (¼ pint) water
350 g (12 oz) butter
700 g (1½ lb) soft light brown sugar
700 g (1½ lb) plain flour
1 tablespoon bicarbonate of soda
6 eggs, beaten
2 teaspoons vanilla essence
300 ml (½ pint) soured cream
Frosting:
225 g (8 oz) butter
225 g (8 oz) cocoa powder
200 ml (7 fl oz) milk
550 g (1¼ lb) icing sugar, sifted

Grease and line the bases of four 23- to 25-cm (9- to 10-inch) sandwich or shallow cake tins with greaseproof paper.

Break the chocolate into a pan. Add the milk and water and heat gently to melt over a low heat. Cool.

Cream the butter and sugar until pale and fluffy. Sift the flour with the bicarbonate of soda. Fold alternately into the creamed mixture with the eggs. Add the vanilla essence, soured cream and chocolate mixture and stir well.

Divide between the prepared cake tins. Bake in a preheated oven, 190°C/375°F (gas mark 5), for about 25–30 minutes, or until well-risen and firm to the touch. Cool slightly in the tins before turning out.

To prepare the frosting, melt the butter in a heavy-based pan. Add the cocoa powder and cook for 1 minute. Stir in the milk and icing sugar and beat until thick and glossy. Allow to cool and thicken. Use to sandwich the chocolate cake layers together and to frost the top of the cake.

NANETTE

Carrot and Brandy Cake

There are so many types of carrot cake – I try lots of them but always come back to this one. It is very moist and is superb as a dessert served with *crème fraiche* or for tea just plain. I've given a recipe for an optional frosting, but really I think it's gilding the lily.

MAKES ONE 23- TO 25-CM (9- TO 10-INCH) CAKE

225 g (8 oz) carrots, peeled and sliced
6 eggs, separated
225 g (8 oz) sugar
1 heaped tablespoon grated raw carrot
grated rind of 1 large orange
350 g (12 oz) ground almonds
1 tablespoon brandy (or fresh orange juice)
Frosting:
225 g (8 oz) cream cheese
6 tablespoons icing sugar, sifted
2 tablespoons concentrated frozen orange juice

Cook the carrots in boiling water until very soft. Drain and purée in a blender or food processor until smooth.

Beat the egg yolks with the sugar until very pale. Add the carrot purée, grated carrot, orange rind, almonds and brandy or orange juice, blending well. Whisk the egg whites until they stand in stiff peaks and fold into the carrot mixture. Pour into a greased loose-bottomed 23- to 25-cm (9- to 10-inch) spring-form cake tin.

Bake in a preheated oven, 160°C/325°F (gas mark 3), for about 50–60 minutes or until a skewer inserted comes out clean. Cool.

To make the frosting, beat the cream cheese with the icing sugar and orange juice (there is no need to thaw it). Chill before swirling over the top of the cake.

If you have one eye on the clock and a cake to make, then try this High-speed Brown Sugary Cake: Liberally butter a 23-cm (9-inch) springform cake tin and spoon over 225 g (8 oz) brown sugar mixed with ½ teaspoon ground cloves and ½ teaspoon ground cinnamon. Put 4 eggs, 75 g (3 oz) ground almonds, 250 ml (8 fl oz) soured cream, 3 tablespoons plain flour, 225 g (8 oz) cream cheese and 2 tablespoons Grand Marnier in a food processor and blend while counting up to 20. Pour into the tin and bake in a preheated oven, 180°C/350°F (gas mark 4), for 40 minutes. Carefully remove from the tin. Serve warm or cold.

Nanette

SARAH

'Sophie's Choice' Chocolate Mousse Cake

Sophie is a great friend of ours and is one of those brilliant 'effortless' cooks who makes entertaining round the kitchen table take on a new meaning. This recipe was left to her as a 'thank you' present by a happy guest.

MAKES ONE 25-CM (10-INCH) CAKE

4 eggs, separated
equal weight of caster sugar
equal weight of butter
equal weight of unsweetened plain chocolate
1 tablespoon self-raising flour

Line a 25-cm (10-inch) diameter spring-form cake tin with greased foil.

Place the egg yolks in a bowl with the sugar. Beat until thick and pale.

Melt the butter in a heavy-based pan with the chocolate. Add to the creamed egg mixture, mixing well. Fold in the flour.

Whisk the egg whites until they stand in stiff peaks. Fold into the chocolate mixture. Spoon into the prepared cake tin and bake in a preheated oven, 180°C/350°F (gas mark 5), for about 45 minutes, or until well risen and springy. Cool in the tin.

EMMA: I often make this to serve with coffee as a dessert.

EMMA

Walnut Cake

MAKES ONE 20-CM (8-INCH) ROUND CAKE

250 ml (8 fl oz) double cream
2 eggs, lightly beaten
225 g (8 oz) caster sugar
50 g (2 oz) ground walnuts
150 g (5 oz) plain flour
2 teaspoons baking powder
pinch of salt
Topping:
25 g (1 oz) butter
1 tablespoon double cream
60 g (2½ oz) caster sugar
1 tablespoon flour
25 g (1 oz) walnuts, coarsely chopped

Whip the cream until it stands in soft peaks. Gradually add the eggs and sugar, beating all the time. Stir in the walnuts. Sift the flour with the baking powder and salt and fold into the creamed mixture.

Pour into a greased and floured 20-cm (8-inch) diameter spring-form cake tin. Bake in a preheated oven, 180°C/350°F (gas mark 4), for 1–1¼ hours, it should feel firm and springy.

To make the topping, melt the butter with the cream, sugar, flour and walnuts in a small pan. Remove the cake from the oven and pour over the walnut mixture to cover. Return to the oven to cook for a further 10 minutes.

Cool slightly in the tin before removing.

Stay For Tea

SARAH

American-style Citrus Cake

I am fortunate enough to have a lemon tree growing in my garden so I can't wait to use the lemons for cooking. I serve this cake with my own home-made lemonade.

MAKES ONE 20-CM (8-INCH) SANDWICH CAKE

Cake:
175 g (6 oz) butter
175 g (6 oz) caster sugar
3 eggs, beaten
finely-grated rind of 1 lemon
175 g (6 oz) self-raising flour
Filling:
3 tablespoons cornflour
3 tablespoons lemon juice
150 g (5 oz) caster sugar
125 ml (4½ fl oz) orange juice
finely-grated rind of 1 lemon
15 g (½ oz) butter
3 egg yolks, lightly beaten
150 ml (¼ pint) double cream
1 lemon, thinly sliced

Grease and line the bases of two 20-cm (8-inch) sandwich tins with greaseproof paper.

Cream the butter with the sugar until pale and fluffy. Add the eggs, a little at a time, mixing well. Fold in the lemon rind and flour. Divide the mixture between the prepared tins and bake in a preheated oven, 190°C/375°F (gas mark 5), for 20 minutes, until firm to the touch. Cool slightly in the tins then transfer to a wire rack.

To make the filling, mix the cornflour with the lemon juice. Place the sugar, orange juice, lemon rind and butter in a heatproof bowl over a pan of boiling water. Add the cornflour mixture. Cook for 5 minutes, stirring constantly, then cook for a further 10 minutes without stirring. Remove the bowl from the heat and stir in the egg yolks. Return to the heat for a further 5–10 minutes, or until the mixture thickens. Remove from the heat and cool, stirring occasionally.

Use two-thirds of the filling to sandwich the cake layers together. Spread the remaining filling over the top of the cake and swirl with a palette knife.

Whip the cream until it stands in soft peaks. Swirl around the edge of the cake and decorate with lemon slices.

SARAH

Angel Food Cake with Strawberry Sauce

I wanted to make a very non-sickly birthday cake for my daughter's first birthday. I dyed the angel cake a very pale pink and served it surrounded by pink roses and strawberries. I made a fresh strawberry sauce to serve with it instead of cream.

MAKES ONE ANGEL FOOD CAKE

8 egg whites
¼ teaspoon salt
1 teaspoon cream of tartar
1½ teaspoons vanilla essence
275 g (10 oz) caster sugar
175 g (6 oz) plain flour
pink food colouring
Strawberry Sauce:
450 g (1 lb) ripe strawberries, hulled
about 4 tablespoons icing sugar, sifted
orange juice to thin (optional)
whole strawberries and pink roses to decorate

Lightly oil a 1.8-litre (3-pint) deep ring or angel food cake tin and coat with flour.

Whisk the egg whites in a large bowl until foamy but not stiff. Add the salt and cream of tartar and continue to whisk until the mixture stands in soft peaks. Add the vanilla essence and caster sugar, a tablespoon at a time, whisking constantly until the mixture stands in firm glossy mountains.

Sift the flour over the egg mixture and fold in. Tint the mixture pink with food colouring – folding it in and taking care not to lose too much air from the mixture. Spoon into the prepared cake tin and bake in a preheated oven, 160°C/325°F (gas mark 3), for 45–50 minutes, or until a skewer inserted comes out clean. Invert onto a wire cooling rack and leave until cold without removing the tin.

When cold, carefully loosen the edges of the cake with a knife and turn out onto a serving plate.

To make the sauce, purée the strawberries in a blender. Beat in icing sugar to taste to make a smooth sauce. If the mixture is a bit thick add a little orange juice to thin it. Just before serving pour the strawberry sauce over the cake and allow to drizzle down the sides. Decorate with fresh whole strawberries and pink roses.

This cake is best eaten on the day of making.

EMMA: For a Hallowe'en Party try tinting the cake with a few drops of green colouring instead of pink. Top with novelty spiders and a liquorice-strand web or anything that makes you go ugh!

EMMA

Apple Sauce Cake

MAKES ONE 19-CM (7½-INCH) SANDWICH CAKE

225 g (8 oz) plain flour
1½ teaspoons bicarbonate of soda
½ teaspoon salt
2 teaspoons ground cinnamon
¼ teaspoon ground nutmeg
150 g (5 oz) butter
225 g (8 oz) caster sugar
2 eggs, beaten
225 g (8 oz) apple purée or canned apple sauce
40 g (1½ oz) sultanas
40 g (1½ oz) raisins
75 g (3 oz) walnuts, coarsely chopped
Frosting:
100 g (4 oz) ricotta cheese
75 g (3 oz) icing sugar, sifted
juice of 1 lime

Grease and line the bases of two 19-cm (7½-inch) sandwich tins with greaseproof paper.

Sift the flour with the bicarbonate of soda, salt, cinnamon and nutmeg. Cream the butter with the sugar until pale and fluffy. Beat in the eggs, a little at a time, adding a small amount of the flour if the mixture begins to curdle. Fold in the remaining flour with the apple purée, sultanas, raisins and walnuts. Divide and spoon into the cake tins.

Bake in a preheated oven, 180°C/350°F (gas mark 4), for 30 minutes, or until well-risen and firm. Cool for a few minutes then turn out onto a wire rack.

For the frosting, beat the ricotta until smooth and creamy. Gradually add the icing sugar with the lime juice, beating all the time to make a smooth frosting.

Sandwich the apple sauce cake layers together with the frosting.

APPLE SAUCE CAKE

SARAH

Boston Cream Pie

This is Pauline's recipe – it's an American one with an English twist.

MAKES ONE 19-CM (7½-INCH) SANDWICH CAKE

Cake:
250 g (9 oz) plain flour
25 g (1 oz) cornflour
2 teaspoons baking powder
½ teaspoon salt
75 g (3 oz) butter
200 g (7 oz) caster sugar
2 eggs, separated
100 ml (4 fl oz) milk
1 teaspoon vanilla essence
Filling:
100 g (4 oz) caster sugar
40 g (1½ oz) plain flour
pinch of salt
300 ml (½ pint) milk
2 egg yolks
2 teaspoons vanilla essence
150 ml (¼ pint) double cream
a sprinkling of icing sugar

Grease and line the bases of two 19-cm (7½-inch) sandwich tins with greaseproof paper.

Sift the flour with the cornflour, baking powder and salt. Cream the butter with the sugar until pale and fluffy. Beat in the egg yolks. Mix the milk with the vanilla essence and stir into the creamed mixture alternately with the flour mixture. Whisk the egg whites until they stand stiffly and fold into the creamed mixture. Spoon into the cake tins.

Bake in a preheated oven, 180°C/350°F (gas mark 4), for 30 minutes, or until a skewer inserted comes out clean.

To make the filling, mix the sugar with the flour and salt. Heat the milk in a pan until hot then gradually add to the flour mixture. Return to the pan and bring to the boil, stirring and cook for 1 minute until smooth and thickened. Beat in the egg yolks and cook, over a low heat, for about 3 minutes. Remove from the heat and stir in the vanilla essence. Cool, stirring now and then. Fold in the cream, whipped until thick.

Sandwich the sponge cake layers with the filling and dust liberally with sifted icing sugar.

EMMA

Double Chocolate Hazelnut Brownies

Originally I had these in America, but I have now created my own version. I can't say it is a recipe that I cook often, simply because it is fatal if you are trying to diet – they are extremely more-ish! They are also useful to keep in the freezer as an emergency pudding.

MAKES ABOUT 16 BROWNIES

75 g (3 oz) butter, softened
50 g (2 oz) bitter or unsweetened chocolate
225 g (8 oz) caster sugar
2 eggs, beaten
½ teaspoon vanilla essence
75 g (3 oz) plain flour
50 g (2 oz) toasted hazelnuts, chopped
50 g (2 oz) chocolate chips

Melt the butter and chocolate over a low heat. Remove from the heat and add the sugar, eggs and vanilla essence, mixing together well. Fold in the flour and spoon into a greased 20-cm (8-inch) square cake tin. Sprinkle with the hazelnuts and chocolate chips, pressing them lightly into the top of the brownie mixture.

Bake in a preheated oven, 180°C/350°F (gas mark 4), for about 30–35 minutes. Cool then cut into squares.

SARAH

Soured Cream Pound Cake

I once ran out of the double cream this recipe usually calls for, so I used soured cream instead. It's much better and makes a wonderful dessert if served with ice cream and surrounded with fresh berries.

MAKES ONE 900-G (2-LB) LOAF, SMALL TUBE OR BUNDT CAKE

100 g (4 oz) butter
100 g (4 oz) sugar
4 eggs, separated
350 g (12 oz) plain flour
pinch of salt
½ teaspoon cream of tartar
150 ml (¼ pint) soured cream mixed with
1 teaspoon vanilla essence

Grease a 900-g (2-lb) loaf tin, small tube or Bundt tin and dust lightly with flour.

Cream the butter with the sugar until pale. Add the egg yolks, one at a time, beating them in well. Sift the flour with the salt and cream of tartar and fold into the creamed mixture alternating with the soured cream.

Whisk the egg whites until they stand in stiff mountains. Fold into the cake mixture. Spoon into the prepared tin and bake in a preheated oven, 180°C/350°F (gas mark 4), for 1¼–1½ hours, or until a skewer inserted comes out clean. Cool on a wire rack.

NANETTE

Celebration Cake

I made both my daughters' wedding cakes. I made them from this recipe (one of my mother's handed down in turn from her mother). This quantity makes a 25-cm (10-inch) deep round cake, so if you were making a wedding cake you would have to work out the sizes (and number of cakes) needed and adjust the recipe accordingly.

Sarah's cake was two-tiered with the top covered in violets and trailing violet ribbons. Emma's was four-tiered – each tier resting on the one below. At the base and between each tier I arranged masses of gypsophila, and on the top more gypsophila with champagne-coloured roses and again trailing ribbons. This is a very effective way of making a cake look beautiful – real flowers, some leaves and lots of ribbons – and forget all those stereotyped decorations.

I make the cake for birthdays and Christmas and it's always a success. Try it, you won't be disappointed.

MAKES ONE 25-CM (10-INCH) ROUND CAKE

350 g (12 oz) plain flour
2 teaspoons ground mixed spice
1 teaspoon freshly ground black pepper
1 teaspoon ground cinnamon
1.25 kg (2½ lb) mixed dried fruit
225 g (8 oz) glacé fruit (use whole glacé fruit and chop it yourself rather than the ready-chopped red and green variety)
100 g (4 oz) walnuts, chopped
50 g (2 oz) flaked almonds
grated rind of 1 orange
grated rind of 1 lemon
275 g (10 oz) butter
275 g (10 oz) caster sugar
8 eggs
small wineglass of rum or brandy

Line a 25-cm (10-inch) round cake tin with greased greaseproof paper.

Sift the flour with the spice, pepper and cinnamon. Add the mixed fruit, glacé fruit, walnuts, almonds and orange and lemon rinds.

Cream the butter with the sugar until pale and fluffy. Beat in the eggs, one at a time. Fold in the dry ingredients and rum or brandy.

Spoon into the prepared cake tin. Bake in a preheated oven, 120°C/250°F (gas mark ½), for 3–4 hours, or until a skewer inserted into the centre of the cake comes out clean. Allow to cool slightly in the tin then turn out onto a wire rack to cool.

Store wrapped in foil in an airtight tin for several weeks to mature.

NANETTE: I always make this type of cake well ahead of time then, every few days, I prod the base with a skewer and pour over a little brandy (or quite a bit of brandy). By the time the cake is ready for eating it is sensational. Don't have a slice before driving!

Try using less fruit and more nuts (Brazils are good) if you prefer a nuttier cake.

CELEBRATION CAKE

NANETTE

The Best Fruit Cake

After my mother died I came across a well-worn copy of *Mrs Beeton* among her books. It had lots of scribbled notes alongside the recipes and handwritten favourites of my mother's own invention. This fruit cake was one of them. She had written across the bottom of the recipe 'The Best Fruit Cake' – I still agree with that.

MAKES ONE 25-CM (10-INCH) ROUND CAKE

1.4 kg (3 lb) mixed dried fruit
175 ml (6 fl oz) dark rum
225 g (8 oz) butter
225 g (8 oz) soft dark brown sugar
5 eggs, separated
225 g (8 oz) self-raising flour
75 g (3 oz) treacle or golden syrup
50 ml (2 fl oz) orange juice
50 g (2 oz) dates, coarsely chopped
100 g (4 oz) walnuts, coarsely chopped

Grease and line a 25-cm (10-inch) round cake tin with a double piece of greaseproof paper. Mix the fruit with the rum, cover and leave to marinate overnight.

Cream the butter with the sugar until light and fluffy. Add the egg yolks, beating well, alternating with the flour. Heat the treacle or golden syrup with the orange juice in a small pan until melted. Stir into the creamed mixture with the dates and walnuts.

Whisk the egg whites until just stiff (don't overbeat) and fold into the fruit mixture. Pour into the prepared cake tin and level the surface. Bake in a preheated oven, 160°C/325°F (gas mark 3), for 2–2½ hours, checking after 2 hours. It's cooked when a skewer inserted into the centre of the cake comes out clean.

When you've taken the cake out of the oven, spoon some extra rum over it while it's still warm. Keeps for ages in an airtight tin.

NANETTE

No-nonsense Lemon and Rice Cake

A plain cake with a great taste – it can be sliced and buttered but I think it's best left alone.

MAKES ONE 15-CM (6-INCH) SQUARE CAKE

100 g (4 oz) butter
200 g (7 oz) caster sugar
grated rind of 2 lemons
2 egg yolks
175 g (6 oz) self-raising flour
50 g (2 oz) ground rice
juice of 1 lemon

Line a 15-cm (6-inch) square cake tin with greaseproof paper.

Cream the butter with the sugar and lemon rind until light and fluffy. Beat in the egg yolks with 4 tablespoons of the flour. Fold in the remaining flour with the ground rice and lemon juice.

Spoon into the prepared tin and bake in a preheated oven, 180°C/350°F (gas mark 4), for 60–70 minutes, or until a skewer inserted comes out clean. Cool in the tin then turn out.

NANETTE

With-anything Biscuits

These are good on their own or spread with butter, Marmite or with cheese.

MAKES ABOUT 20 BISCUITS

100 g (4 oz) plain wholemeal flour
1 teaspoon ground coriander
60 g (2½ oz) butter
25 g (1 oz) rolled oats
3 tablespoons natural yoghurt

Sift the flour with the coriander, adding any bran left in the sieve. Rub in the butter until the mixture resembles fine breadcrumbs. Stir in the oats and yoghurt and mix to a smooth dough.

Roll out quite thinly on a lightly-floured surface and cut into about 20 squares. Prick with a fork and place on lightly-greased baking trays.

Bake in a preheated oven, 200°C/400°F (gas mark 6), for 10–15 minutes, or until crisp and firm. Cool on a wire rack. Store in an airtight tin.

Nothing tastes better than your own home-made lemon curd. It is simple to make and is delicious on toast, in tarts or over ice cream. Gently cook 6 lightly-beaten egg yolks with 225 g (8 oz) caster sugar and 100 ml (4 fl oz) freshly-squeezed lemon juice until the mixture coats the back of a spoon. Stir all the time to keep the mixture smooth. Gradually beat in 100 g (4 oz) softened butter then pot in sterilised jars. Seal, label and store in the refrigerator for up to 3 weeks.

Nanette

SARAH

Peanut Butter Cookies

MAKES ABOUT 30 COOKIES

350 g (12 oz) butter
100 g (4 oz) soft light brown sugar
150 g (5 oz) granulated sugar
175 g (6 oz) crunchy peanut butter
1 egg, beaten
150 g (5 oz) plain flour
½ teaspoon baking powder
½ teaspoon vanilla essence

Cream the butter with the sugars and peanut butter until light and fluffy. Beat in the egg, mixing well. Sift the flour with the baking powder and fold into the creamed mixture with the vanilla essence. Shape into a long roll about 4 cm (1½ inches) in diameter. Wrap in clingfilm and chill until firm.

Unwrap the cookie mixture and slice thinly into about 30 rounds. Place well apart on lightly-greased baking trays. Bake in a preheated oven, 180°C/350°F (gas mark 4), for 12–15 minutes, or until crisp and golden. Cool on a wire rack.

They keep well if they get the chance.

NANETTE

Pistachio Cookies

MAKES ABOUT 20

100 g (4 oz) butter
100 g (4 oz) light brown sugar
1 egg
100 g (4 oz) plain flour
½ teaspoon vanilla essence
75 g (3 oz) pistachio nuts

Cream the butter with the sugar. Beat in the egg until well mixed. Fold in the flour, then add the vanilla essence and pistachio nuts, stirring well.

Place small mounds of the mixture (about the size of a dessertspoon) on greased baking trays, spacing well apart. Bake in a preheated oven, 190°C/375°F (gas mark 5), for about 12 minutes, or until pale brown and cooked. Cool on a wire rack.

Gillian's Lemon Loaf is so good that you must try it – now! Sift 250 g (9 oz) plain flour with ½ teaspoon salt and 1½ teaspoons baking powder. Stir in 350 g (12 oz) caster sugar. Place this mixture and 175 g (6 oz) butter in a food processor and whirl to mix. Add 3 beaten eggs, 175 ml (6 fl oz) milk and whirl quickly to just mix (don't overmix). Pour into a lightly-greased 900-g (2-lb) loaf tin and bake in a preheated oven, 180°C/350°F (gas mark 4), for 1¼ hours. Allow to cool for 10 minutes then turn out onto a cooling rack and brush with this glaze: Bring 6 tablespoons lemon juice and 25 g (1 oz) sugar to the boil and cook for 3 minutes. Brush over the cake.

Nanette

EMMA

Utterly Simple Biscuits

This is a really good biscuit recipe because you can add things to it to ring the changes – try adding some chopped nuts, or a teaspoon of ground ginger instead of the orange essence, a little desiccated coconut or grated lemon rind.

MAKES ABOUT 20 BISCUITS

175 g (6 oz) butter
275 g (10 oz) sugar
2 egg whites
225 g (8 oz) plain flour
2 tablespoons cornflour
1 teaspoon orange essence

Cream the butter with the sugar until thick and pale. Beat the egg whites until foamy then beat into the butter mixture.

Sift the flour with the cornflour and fold into the creamed mixture with the orange essence, blending well to make a dough. Divide and roll into about 20 walnut-sized balls. Place well apart on two lightly-greased baking trays and flatten slightly with your thumb.

Bake in a preheated oven, 180°C/350°F (gas mark 4), for about 20 minutes, or until pale brown.

SARAH: I make these biscuits but refrigerate the dough and simply slice off and bake as many biscuits as I need at any one time. The dough will keep in the refrigerator for 3–4 days if wrapped in clingfilm or foil – they taste doubly delicious if baked fresh daily.

EMMA

Lumpy Biscuits

This is a recipe from my childhood. My mother made them when I had friends for tea. They're still my favourite and everyone always likes them. They are mis-shapen, so they *look* home-made.

MAKES ABOUT 20 BISCUITS

100 g (4 oz) plain flour
½ teaspoon baking powder
100 g (4 oz) butter
175 g (6 oz) soft dark brown sugar
50 g (2 oz) caster sugar
1 egg, beaten
1 tablespoon natural yoghurt
100 g (4 oz) jumbo oats

Sift the flour with the baking powder. Cream the butter with the sugars until pale and fluffy. Beat in the egg and yoghurt, mixing well. Add the flour, half at a time, then fold in the oats, mixing well.

Drop tablespoonfuls of the mixture onto greased baking trays (well apart because they spread) and bake in a preheated oven, 180°C/350°F (gas mark 4), for 12–14 minutes, or until pale brown and cooked. Cool on a wire rack.

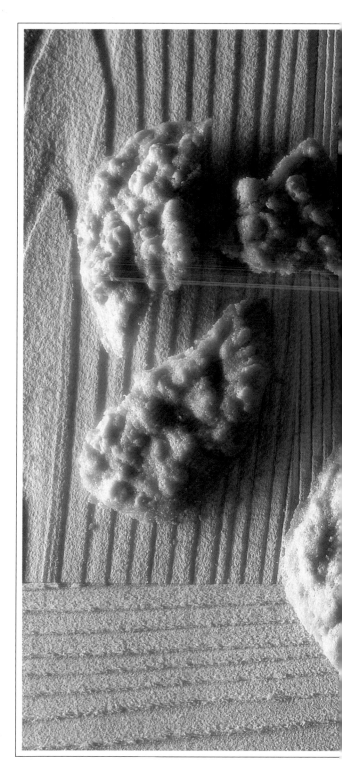

LUMPY BISCUITS

Evenings In

Eating in the evening is a movable feast – an informal dinner party, early meal with the children, late night supper or merely something on a tray while watching the latest soap on television. Whatever or wherever it is, here are some suggestions.

Nanette

SARAH

Black Bean Soup

SERVES 6–8

1.25 kg (2½ lb) black beans, soaked overnight in cold water
1.2 litres (2 pints) beef stock
1.2 litres (2 pints) water
100 g (4 oz) lean back bacon, rinded
1 ham bone (optional)
25 g (1 oz) unsalted butter
1 onion, peeled and chopped
1 carrot, peeled and chopped
2 small leeks, chopped
50 g (2 oz) celery tops, chopped
small bunch of fresh parsley
pinch of dried thyme
1 bay leaf
freshly ground black pepper
salt
soured cream to serve

Rinse and drain the beans in cold water and put them in a large pan. Add the stock, water, bacon and ham bone. Bring to the boil, reduce the heat and simmer while preparing the vegetables.

Melt the butter in a pan, add the onion, carrot, leeks, celery tops and a few sprigs of parsley. Cook, over a gentle heat, until softened. Add to the soup with the thyme, bay leaf and pepper to taste. Cover and simmer until the beans are very soft and tender, stirring occasionally. This will take about 3 hours.

Remove the bacon, bay leaf and ham bone. Thin the soup with beef stock if liked (personally, I find the texture perfect). Taste and adjust the seasoning with salt and pepper.

Serve the soup piping hot with a spoonful of soured cream.

EMMA

Main Course Soup

This is another recipe that I have stolen from my friend Angela. It's absolutely delicious and very filling – a meal in itself.

SERVES 6–8

225 g (8 oz) dried red kidney or haricot beans, soaked overnight and then drained
100 g (4 oz) salt pork, diced
2 cloves of garlic, peeled and finely chopped
1 Spanish onion, peeled and quartered
4 carrots, peeled and finely sliced
4 sticks of celery, finely chopped
1.2 litres (2 pints) beef stock
½ small head of cabbage, coarsely shredded
4 leaves of curly endive, coarsely shredded
4 tomatoes, skinned and coarsely chopped
225 g (8 oz) green beans, topped and tailed and coarsely chopped
100 g (4 oz) frozen peas
100 g (4 oz) short-cut macaroni
salt
freshly ground black pepper
2 tablespoons chopped fresh parsley
2 tablespoons olive oil
4 tablespoons freshly-grated Parmesan cheese

Cook the beans in boiling salted water until tender, about 2 hours. Drain and set aside.

Dry-fry the salt pork in a heavy-based frying pan until golden. Add the garlic and onion and cook until softened. Transfer to a large saucepan, stir in the carrots, celery and stock. Bring to the boil, reduce the heat and simmer for 10 minutes.

Add the cabbage, endive, tomatoes, green beans and cooked beans. Bring to the boil, reduce the heat, cover and simmer for 1½ hours until tender.

Stir in the frozen peas and macaroni with salt and pepper to taste. Bring to the boil, reduce the heat and simmer until the macaroni is tender, about 15 minutes.

Stir in the parsley and olive oil. Serve hot sprinkled with the freshly-grated Parmesan cheese. Serve piping hot with chunks of interesting bread.

MAIN COURSE SOUP

Evenings In

Trout Kedgeree

This is a simple dish and very quick to make if you have all the ingredients ready beforehand.

SERVES 4

225 g (8 oz) long-grain rice
50 g (2 oz) butter
1 bunch of spring onions, trimmed and chopped
225 g (8 oz) smoked trout, boned and flaked
3 hard-boiled eggs, shelled and chopped
1 bunch of watercress, trimmed and finely chopped
salt
freshly ground black pepper
3 tablespoons double cream
2 tablespoons toasted flaked almonds

Cook the rice in boiling salted water until tender. Drain thoroughly.

Melt the butter in a large shallow pan, add the spring onions and sauté until tender, about 5 minutes (do not allow to brown). Mix in the rice and trout and cook until hot.

Add the eggs, watercress and salt and pepper. Stir in the cream and almonds and cook for 1–2 minutes until hot. Serve at once.

Seafood Supper

SERVES 4

1 tablespoon sunflower oil
1 onion, peeled and finely chopped
½ green pepper, cored, seeded and sliced
½ red pepper, cored, seeded and sliced
225 g (8 oz) long-grain brown rice
large pinch of turmeric or powdered saffron
600–900 ml (1–1½ pints) fish stock
550 g (1¼ lb) mixed cooked shelled shellfish (for example, prawns, shrimps, crab, lobster, mussels, clams or oysters)
salt
freshly ground black pepper
2 tablespoons chopped fresh parsley

Heat the oil in a large shallow pan. Add the onion and sauté until softened. Stir in the peppers, rice and turmeric or saffron and cook for 2 minutes, stirring constantly.

Add sufficient stock to cover the rice mixture. Cover and simmer for 25 minutes, stirring occasionally. Pour in a little more stock if the mixture begins to cook dry.

Stir in the prepared shellfish with salt and pepper. Cover and cook for a further 5 minutes or until the shellfish are hot and the rice is cooked and all the stock has been absorbed.

Stir in the parsley and serve.

I don't use anything that can't go into the dishwasher. However pretty the design, if it can't go into the machine, I don't buy it. I have the same shapes of plates and cups in different colours. I mix them up, and if one gets broken, it doesn't matter, it's easily replaceable. I love large cups of coffee after dinner, mine are extra large.

Sarah

NANETTE

Friday Fish Pie

SERVES 4

700 g (1½ lb) white fish fillets (cod or haddock, for example)

salt

freshly ground white pepper

1 bay leaf

150 ml (¼ pint) water

40 g (1½ oz) butter

25 g (1 oz) flour

150 ml (¼ pint) milk

100 g (4 oz) frozen peas

2 tablespoons chopped fresh parsley

1 tablespoon chopped fresh tarragon

pinch of ground nutmeg

100 g (4 oz) peeled prawns

2 tablespoons double cream

Topping:

50 g (2 oz) butter

75 g (3 oz) fresh breadcrumbs

25 g (1 oz) hazelnuts, chopped

50 g (2 oz) Cheddar cheese, grated

Place the fish fillets in a buttered ovenproof dish and season with salt and pepper. Add the bay leaf and water, cover with foil and bake in a preheated oven, 160°C/325°F (gas mark 3), for 15 minutes or until the fish is tender. Skin and flake the fish, reserving the cooking juices.

Melt the butter in a pan. Add the flour, blending well and cook for 1 minute. Gradually add the milk and 150 ml (¼ pint) of the reserved cooking juices, stirring well. Bring to the boil, stirring constantly, and cook until smooth and thickened. Remove from the heat and add the peas, parsley, tarragon, nutmeg and salt and pepper. Fold in the prawns, flaked fish and cream. Spoon into a medium buttered pie or gratin dish.

To make the topping, melt the butter in a heavy-based frying pan. Add the breadcrumbs and stir around until golden. Remove from the heat, stir in the hazelnuts and cheese. Sprinkle over the fish mixture. Cook under a preheated hot grill until bubbly, about 2 minutes.

Serve at once with grilled or baked tomato halves.

EMMA: As an alternative, replace the peas with asparagus tips.

SARAH

Turkey and Pumpkin Pie

SERVES 6

12 baby button onions, peeled
450 ml (¾ pint) water
2 tablespoons cornflour
150 ml (¼ pint) milk
75 g (3 oz) Cheddar cheese, grated
salt
freshly ground black pepper
450 g (1 lb) cooked turkey, chopped
350 g (12 oz) slice of pumpkin, peeled, seeded and cubed
2 tablespoons chopped fresh parsley
250 g (8¾ oz) packet frozen puff pastry, thawed
beaten egg to glaze

Cook the onions in the water until just tender, about 8–10 minutes. Mix the cornflour with the milk and blend into the onion mixture. Bring to the boil, stirring constantly, until smooth and thick. Add the cheese and salt and pepper. Fold in the turkey, pumpkin and parsley. Spoon into a 1.2-litre (2-pint) pie dish.

Roll out the pastry to an oval or round about 4 cm (1½ inches) larger than the pie dish. Trim a 2.5-cm (1-inch) strip from the edge of the pastry to make a pastry collar. Moisten the pie dish rim with water and press the pastry collar firmly on to the rim, overlapping the ends. Dampen the pastry collar with water then top with the pastry lid and press firmly together. Trim away any excess pastry and knock up the crust to seal. Flute the edges of the pie and decorate with any pastry trimmings. Glaze with beaten egg.

Bake in a preheated oven, 220°C/425°F (gas mark 7), for about 25–30 minutes, or until the pastry is well-risen and golden and the filling is piping hot. Serve at once with jacket potatoes and a green vegetable.

Evenings In

SARAH

Chicken Burgers

I don't like my children eating red meat, so I invented these burgers for a birthday party treat. I managed to kill quite a few birds with one stone with this recipe because you can cram hidden vegetables and fibre into them – grown-ups also fight for the leftovers! Serve them with miniature wholewheat buns, a little mayonnaise and ketchup and children will forget that McDonald's ever existed!

SERVES 6 CHILDREN OR 4 ADULTS

700 g (1½ lb) lean chicken or turkey, minced
2 carrots, peeled and grated
2 courgettes, trimmed and grated
¼ onion, peeled and grated
2 tablespoons chopped fresh parsley
3 tablespoons tomato ketchup
1 tablespoon bran or wheatgerm
3 tablespoons oatmeal
salt
freshly ground black pepper
4–6 tablespoons dried breadcrumbs
2 tablespoons sunflower oil

Mix the chicken or turkey with the carrots, courgettes, onion, parsley, tomato ketchup, bran or wheatgerm, oatmeal and salt and pepper. Divide and shape into about 12 small patties. Coat in the breadcrumbs and chill for 15 minutes.

To cook, heat the oil in a large frying pan and sauté the chicken burgers until golden and crisp, about 3–4 minutes on each side. Drain on absorbent paper.

Serve hot in miniature wholewheat buns, topped with a little mayonnaise and ketchup.

EMMA

Easy Casserole

This is an easy casserole to prepare if you're out at work all day. Cook in a slow-cooker or on a very low heat in the oven from early morning, so that you have something warm to come home to in the evening.

SERVES 4–6

1 kg (2 lb) lean stewing beef, cut into cubes
1 tablespoon plain flour
2 tablespoons vegetable oil
1 onion, peeled and sliced or 2 large leeks,
washed and sliced
450 g (1 lb) button mushrooms, wiped
4 courgettes, trimmed and chopped
3 large carrots, peeled and chopped
295 g (10 oz) can beef consommé
450 ml (¾ pint) beef stock
salt
freshly ground black pepper

Lightly coat the beef with the flour. Heat the oil in a large pan, add the meat, in batches, and brown on all sides. Remove the meat from the pan and place in a large casserole or slow cooker.

Add the onion or leeks to the pan and sauté until softened. Add the mushrooms and cook for a further 1 minute. Transfer to the casserole and add the courgettes, carrots, beef consommé, stock and salt and pepper.

Cook in a preheated oven, 180°C/350°F (gas mark 4), for 2–2½ hours; in a cool oven, 140°C/275°F (gas mark 1), for 8–10 hours, or in a slow cooker, until the meat and vegetables are tender.

Serve hot on a bed of brown or white rice.

NANETTE

Bryan's Beef Goulash

Coming home tired after a day at the studio, I was not looking forward to the prospect of preparing dinner. Imagine my amazement, and delight, when I was greeted by a fugitive from a word processor who announced that dinner would be served in half an hour. With a mixture of pride, fear and exhaustion, Bryan told me he'd been preparing the feast since early morning (he is not a fast-order cook). When I asked him how he had suddenly acquired his culinary skills, he flattered me by saying he had watched me over the years – a kitchen *voyeur*.

In the event, by candlelight, with wine and all the trimmings, I enjoyed his Rolls Royce goulash – which by his own calculation had cost a fortune (by mistake he'd bought the best fillet steak and made enough for 8). It can be made much cheaper – provided you don't hire Bryan. It's especially delicious if you don't have to cook it yourself!

SERVES 4

1 tablespoon plain flour
1 teaspoon ground paprika
1 kg (2 lb) chuck steak, cut into cubes
3 tablespoons sunflower oil
2 cloves of garlic, peeled and chopped
2 large onions, peeled and sliced
2 large carrots, peeled and thinly sliced
2 red peppers, cored, seeded and sliced
400 g (14 oz) can tomatoes
1 teaspoon dried oregano
150 ml (¼ pint) beef stock
150 ml (¼ pint) red wine
salt
freshly ground black pepper
finely-grated rind of 1 lemon

Mix the flour with the paprika and use to lightly coat the meat cubes. Heat the oil in a large pan, add the meat and brown on all sides. Remove the meat from the pan with a slotted spoon and place in a large casserole.

Add the garlic, onions, carrots and peppers to the pan juices and sauté gently for 5 minutes. Add the tomatoes with their juice, oregano, stock, red wine and salt and pepper. Cook for 2 minutes then add to the casserole.

Cook in a preheated oven, 180°C/350°F (gas mark 4), for about 2 hours, or until the meat and vegetables are fork tender – checking after 1 hour cooking time. Ten minutes before serving add the lemon rind. Serve hot with soured cream, rice and salad.

Evenings In

EMMA

Shepherd's Pie with Layers

When Sarah and I were living at home we always looked forward to the weekends. The house would be full of family and friends and the kitchen was like Waterloo Station. We were given jobs and, as we became more reliable, allowed to invent and cook our own dishes. I'm sure some of them must have been awful but we were always encouraged. My mother used to say there was method in her madness, since she knew one day we would become good cooks and she and Daddy would be coming to our homes for dinner. I'm glad to say that happens a lot. This is something I often serve.

SERVES 4

2 teaspoons vegetable oil
1 onion, peeled and chopped
700 g (1½ lb) lean minced beef
400 g (14 oz) can peeled plum tomatoes, coarsely chopped
1 teaspoon yeast extract
1 beef stock cube, crumbled
salt
freshly ground black pepper
300 g (10 oz) packet frozen creamed spinach
450 g (1 lb) carrots, peeled and sliced
1 tablespoon double cream
450 g (1 lb) peeled potatoes
15 g (½ oz) butter
1–2 tablespoons milk
50 g (2 oz) Cheddar cheese, grated

Heat the oil in a pan, add the onion and sauté until softened. Stir in the beef and cook until well browned and no longer pink. Add the tomatoes, yeast extract, stock cube and salt and pepper. Bring to the boil, reduce the heat, cover and simmer for 30 minutes or thereabouts.

Cook the spinach according to the packet instructions and set aside. Cook the carrots in boiling salted water until tender. Drain and purée with the cream and salt and pepper.

Cook the potatoes in boiling salted water until tender. Drain and mash with the butter and milk until creamy.

Place the beef mixture in the base of a large deep ovenproof dish. Top with the spinach and layer evenly. Cover with the creamed carrot and finally top with the creamed potatoes. Sprinkle with the grated cheese.

Bake in a preheated oven, 200°C/400°F (gas mark 6), for about 30–40 minutes, or until the top has crisped up and turned pale brown.

SARAH

Newley's Meat Loaf

Tony and Dareth are great friends. She is a great cook and here is her 'great' meat loaf.

SERVES 8

3 egg yolks
3 tablespoons water
25 g (1 oz) porridge oats
1.4 kg (3 lb) lean minced beef
2 carrots, peeled and grated
1 large onion, peeled and finely chopped
1 clove of garlic, peeled and crushed (optional)
3 tablespoons tomato ketchup
2 tablespoons wholegrain French mustard
2 tablespoons chopped fresh parsley
2 tablespoons chopped fresh mixed herbs (for example, rosemary, thyme, sage, chives and chervil)
2 teaspoons lemon juice
pinch of chilli powder
2 teaspoons salt
1 teaspoon freshly ground black pepper
227 g (8 oz) can chilli sauce or

Home-made Tomato Topping:
227 g (8 oz) can tomatoes, drained and chopped
2 tablespoons tomato purée
2 tablespoons soft brown sugar
1 tablespoon cider vinegar
1 tablespoon made mustard
2 tablespoons chopped fresh parsley

Stir the egg yolks with the water and oats and leave to stand for 10 minutes.

Mix the beef with the carrots, onion, garlic, if used, tomato ketchup, mustard, parsley, herbs, lemon juice, oat mixture, chilli powder and salt and pepper. Place on a very lightly greased baking tray and shape into a loaf. Top with the chilli sauce or Home-made Tomato Topping. Prepare the tomato topping by mixing the ingredients in a small pan. Bring to the boil, reduce the heat and simmer until thick and pulpy, about 10–15 minutes.

Bake in a preheated oven, 180°C/350°F (gas mark 4), for 1½ hours until cooked. Serve hot with creamy whipped potatoes and steamed broccoli or cold with salad.

NEWLEY'S MEAT LOAF

Evenings In

SARAH

Lasagne with Goat's Cheese and Yoghurt Topping

SERVES 6

2 tablespoons sunflower oil
1 large onion, peeled and chopped
450 g (1 lb) minced beef
400 g (14 oz) can chopped tomatoes
2 tablespoons Worcestershire sauce
1 tablespoon tomato purée
1 teaspoon dried mixed herbs
150 ml (¼ pint) beef stock
salt
freshly ground black pepper
175 g (6 oz) no pre-cook lasagne sheets
225 g (8 oz) round goat's cheese, thinly sliced
450 ml (¾ pint) natural yoghurt
1 tablespoon cornflour
50 g (2 oz) Cheddar cheese, grated
2 tablespoons freshly-grated Parmesan cheese

Heat the oil in a pan. Add the onion and sauté until softened. Add the beef and fry until browned. Add the tomatoes, Worcestershire sauce, tomato purée, herbs, stock and salt and pepper. Cover and simmer for 20 minutes.

Layer the meat sauce with the lasagne and goat's cheese in a greased ovenproof dish, finishing with a layer of pasta.

Mix the yoghurt with the cornflour in a pan. Bring to the boil, stirring until smooth and lightly thickened. Stir in the Cheddar cheese and salt and pepper. Spoon over the lasagne and sprinkle with the Parmesan cheese.

Bake in a preheated oven, 180°C/350°F (gas mark 4), for 45 minutes, until cooked and lightly browned.

Evenings In

EMMA

Vegetarian Rice Dish

This is a dish that I make when all of my favourite vegetables are in season. It is delicious enough to eat on its own.

SERVES 4–6

225 g (8 oz) long-grain brown rice
1 vegetable stock cube
250 ml (8 fl oz) hot water
about 1 kg (2 lb) prepared fresh vegetables (for example, broccoli florets, sliced carrots, trimmed mangetout, wiped mushrooms and fresh sweetcorn kernels)
100 g (4 oz) mature Cheddar cheese, grated
salt
freshly ground black pepper
25 g (1 oz) butter

Cook the rice in boiling salted water, according to the packet instructions, until tender, about 30 minutes. Drain thoroughly. Dissolve the stock cube in the hot water and set aside.

Meanwhile, steam the vegetables until just tender but still crisp. Mix with the rice and place in a large shallow ovenproof dish. Moisten with the stock. Sprinkle with the cheese, season to taste with salt and pepper and dot with the butter.

Bake in a preheated oven, 180°C/350°F (gas mark 4), for 15–20 minutes until the cheese has melted and the rice and vegetable mixture is hot.

EMMA

Spinach and Bacon Bake

This is an easy dish to make and good for preparing on a night when you don't have the energy to make something complicated.

SERVES 4

450 g (1 lb) packet frozen spinach, thawed
4 rashers unsmoked streaky bacon, rinded and chopped
100 g (4 oz) mushrooms, wiped and sliced
salt
freshly ground black pepper
½ teaspoon dried thyme
300 ml (½ pint) soured cream
225 g (8 oz) mature Cheddar cheese, grated
50 g (2 oz) freshly-grated Parmesan cheese

Cook the spinach according to the packet instructions. Drain thoroughly and place in the base of a buttered ovenproof dish.

Fry the bacon until crisp, drain on absorbent paper, crumble and sprinkle over the spinach. Top with the mushrooms, salt, pepper and thyme. Cover and cook in a preheated oven, 190°C/375°F (gas mark 5), for 10 minutes.

Meanwhile, mix the soured cream with the cheeses. Spoon over the spinach and bacon mixture. Return to the oven and cook, uncovered, for a further 10 minutes, or until the cheese topping is melted and bubbly.

Serve at once with unusual breads.

EMMA

Macaroni Cheese with Mushrooms

I have made this more times than I care to remember – but Graham loves it and never seems to mind.

SERVES 4

1 tablespoon olive oil
350 g (12 oz) macaroni
50 g (2 oz) butter
25 g (1 oz) plain flour
600 ml (1 pint) milk
100 g (4 oz) Cheddar or Red Leicester cheese, grated
225 g (8 oz) cooked ham, chopped
100 g (4 oz) button mushrooms, cooked
salt
freshly ground black pepper
3 tomatoes, sliced
2 tablespoons freshly-grated Parmesan cheese

Bring a large pan of water to the boil and add the olive oil and the macaroni. Boil briskly, uncovered, for 8–10 minutes (or according to the packet instructions), until the pasta is cooked *al dente*. Drain thoroughly and set aside.

Melt the butter in a pan. Add the flour, blending well and cook for about 1 minute. Gradually add the milk, bring to the boil, stirring constantly, and cook until thickened.

Remove from the heat and stir in the cheese, ham, mushrooms and salt and pepper.

Place the macaroni in a medium ovenproof dish and pour over the sauce, making sure that it covers all of the pasta. Top with the sliced tomatoes and sprinkle with the Parmesan cheese.

Bake in a preheated oven, 200°C/400°F (gas mark 6), for about 20 minutes. Serve hot with a green salad.

Evenings In

NANETTE

Spaghetti with Uncooked Fresh Tomato Sauce

Some of the best recipes are the simplest. This is from Mariella, who lives in Rome; it is a spaghetti to serve in the summer. The tomatoes must be *very* ripe, and of course the spaghetti must be cooked *al dente*.

SERVES 3

4 very large ripe tomatoes, skinned and very finely chopped
5 tablespoons good-quality olive oil
juice of 1 lemon
3 tablespoons chopped fresh basil
salt
freshly ground black pepper
250 g (9 oz) spaghetti

At least 4 hours before required, mix the tomatoes with 4 tablespoons of the oil, the lemon juice, basil and salt and pepper. Leave to stand, covered, until required.

Bring a large pan of water to the boil and add the remaining olive oil and the spaghetti. Boil briskly, uncovered, for 8–10 minutes (or according to the packet instructions), until the pasta is cooked *al dente*. Drain thoroughly and place in a large warmed serving dish. Add the prepared fresh tomato sauce and toss lightly.

Serve at once with a salad of lettuce hearts.

SARAH

Savoury Crêpe Batter

MAKES ABOUT 16 SMALL OR 8 MEDIUM CRÊPES

100 g (4 oz) plain flour
6 tablespoons milk
6 tablespoons water
3 large eggs (size 1, 2)
pinch of salt
25 g (1 oz) butter, melted

Place the flour, milk, water, eggs and salt in a blender or food processor. Blend until smooth and creamy, scraping the mixture down once during mixing. Cover and leave to stand for 1 hour.

Heat a small heavy-based frying pan over a moderate heat. Brush lightly with a little of the butter. Beat the batter mixture and pour about 2–3 tablespoons into the centre of the pan (depending upon the size of the pan). Tilt the pan immediately so that the batter evenly coats the base. Cook for about 1 minute until lightly browned underneath. Turn over and cook for a further ½ minute. Remove from the pan and stack the crêpes on a plate interleaving greaseproof paper between them to prevent them sticking together. Repeat with the remaining mixture, brushing the pan lightly with butter each time a crêpe is made, until all the batter has been used.

EMMA

Exotic Crêpe Filling with Blue Cheese

SERVES 4

25 g (1 oz) butter
1 onion, peeled and chopped
½ green pepper, cored, seeded and thinly sliced
½ red pepper, cored, seeded and thinly sliced
100 g (4 oz) mushrooms, wiped and sliced
25 g (1 oz) sultanas
25 g (1 oz) unsalted cashew nuts, chopped
175 g (6 oz) cooked gammon or chicken, chopped
225 g (8 oz) beanshoots
salt
freshly ground black pepper
1 recipe Savoury Crêpe Batter (see page 98)
Sauce:
25 g (1 oz) butter
25 g (1 oz) plain flour
300 ml (½ pint) milk
50 g (2 oz) Danish Mellow Blue cheese

Melt the butter in a pan. Add the onion and sauté until softened. Stir in the peppers and mushrooms and cook for 2–3 minutes. Add the sultanas, nuts and gammon or chicken and cook until hot, about 3 minutes. Stir in the beanshoots and salt and pepper.

Fold each crêpe in half and then in half again. Lift up the top layer and generously fill with the beanshoot mixture. Arrange in an ovenproof dish and keep warm.

To make the sauce, melt the butter in a pan. Add the flour and cook for 1 minute. Gradually add the milk, bring to the boil, stirring constantly, until smooth and thickened. Crumble in the cheese and stir until melted. Serve the crêpes with the sauce separately.

Evenings In

NANETTE

Scrambled Egg and Smoked Salmon Crêpe Filling

SERVES 4

6 eggs, lightly beaten

8 tablespoons milk

2 tablespoons chopped fresh herbs (for example, parsley, chives and chervil)

100 g (4 oz) smoked salmon, chopped

salt

freshly ground black pepper

25 g (1 oz) butter

1 recipe Savoury Crêpe Batter (see page 98)

Beat the eggs with the milk, herbs, smoked salmon and salt and pepper. Melt the butter in a heavy-based pan. Add the egg mixture and cook over a gentle heat until the mixture is lightly scrambled and creamy.

Divide the mixture evenly between the warm crêpes and fold over or roll up to enclose. Serve at once.

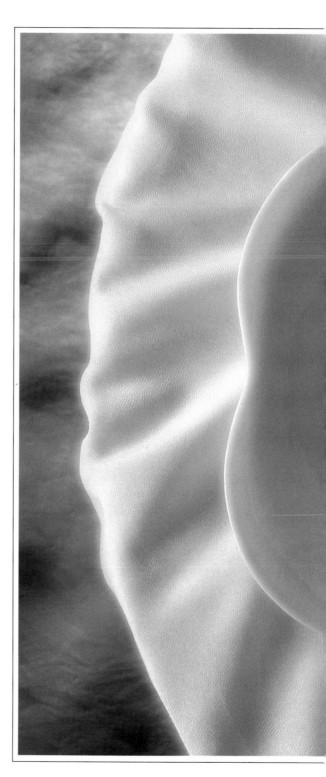

SCRAMBLED EGG AND SMOKED SALMON CRÊPES

Evenings In

NANETTE

Double Cheese and Apple Crêpe Filling

SERVES 4

1 eating apple, peeled, cored and thinly sliced
225 g (8 oz) cottage cheese
2 tablespoons chopped fresh chives
salt
freshly ground black pepper
1 recipe Savoury Crêpe Batter (see page 98)
Sauce:
25 g (1 oz) butter
25 g (1 oz) plain flour
300 ml (½ pint) milk
100 g (4 oz) Cheddar cheese, grated

Mix the apple with the cottage cheese, chives and salt and pepper. Divide the mixture between the crêpes and roll up to enclose. Place, seam-side down, in an ovenproof dish.

To make the sauce, melt the butter in a pan. Add the flour and cook for 1 minute. Gradually add the milk, bring to the boil, stirring constantly, until smooth and thickened. Stir in three-quarters of the grated cheese with salt and pepper until melted.

Pour over the crêpes and sprinkle with the remaining cheese. Bake in a preheated oven, 190°C/375°F (gas mark 5), for 20–25 minutes, or until bubbly and lightly browned. Serve hot with a mixed salad.

Entertaining on a large scale is something most of us do only a few times a year, so – when you do decide on a full-scale party – here are a few tried and tested tips:

☐ Send a map of how to get to your home if it's difficult to find.

☐ If the party is in the evening check how many candles you will need.

☐ Choose your menu and order food well in advance.

☐ Leave the day before as free as you can to do as much pre-cooking as possible, to arrange flowers and lay tables.

☐ If the food is buffet-style then make sure your table looks attractive. I always use a to-the-floor tablecloth (or sheets) with another shorter cloth on top. For Emma's wedding I bought masses of white muslin and laid it over the underneath cloth, letting it billow onto the floor. I then scooped it up at intervals, all around the table, sewed it in place and added flowers, ribbons and trailing leaves – the effect was lovely.

☐ Hiring napkins can be expensive – in fact it can be cheaper to buy plain white ones at the sales. Or opt for double-thickness paper ones.

☐ If you are having a large sit-down dinner party and you don't have any help, have the first course ready on the table, then let guests help themselves to the main course – it is less formal and simpler.

☐ I love giving a party for a reason because then you have something to hang it on. Celebrating something special gives a party an extra fillip – it also gives you a chance to make the occasion memorable.

Nanette

SARAH

Party Pizza

These pizzas are a wonderful way to feed a lot of people with very little effort. No two ever turn out the same, and you can experiment to your heart's content. I usually arrange my different chosen fillings on individual plates and let everyone help to choose and invent the pizza as they go along. Each pizza will serve six people.

SERVES 6

Pizza Dough:
25 g (1 oz) dried yeast
4 teaspoons clear honey
450 ml (¾ pint) lukewarm water
600 g (1 lb 5 oz) plain flour
4 teaspoons salt
2 tablespoons olive oil

Mix the yeast with the honey and 6 tablespoons of the water. Leave to stand in a warm place until frothy (about 10–15 minutes). Mix the flour with the salt, remaining water, oil and yeast mixture and mix to a smooth and pliable dough. Knead for about 10 minutes until smooth and elastic. Cover and leave to prove in a warm place until doubled in size – about 30 minutes.

Divide the dough into three pieces, wrap in a towel or clingfilm and refrigerate for 4 hours. (At this point the dough may be frozen if liked.)

Roll or flatten out each piece of dough into a 30-cm (12-inch) circle and place on a greased pizza pan or baking tray. Cover with your chosen toppings, then bake in a preheated oven, 230°C/450°F (gas mark 8), for 15 minutes. Reduce the oven temperature to 200°C/400°F (gas mark 6), and cook for a further 5 minutes.

Here are two of my favourite fillings:

Spinach, Cherry Tomato, Spring Onion and Feta Cheese Pizza

Brush the pizza base with 1 tablespoon olive oil. Cover with 425 g (15 oz) home-made or canned tomato pizza sauce. Squeeze any excess water from a 275-g (10-oz) packet frozen leaf spinach (thawed) and divide over the sauce. Top with 200 g (7 oz) grated cheese, 12 halved cherry tomatoes, 100 g (4 oz) crumbled Feta cheese, 6 chopped spring onions and salt and pepper to taste. Bake as above.

Pesto, Cheddar, Tomato, Red Onion and Mozzarella with Basil Pizza

Brush the pizza base with 1 tablespoon olive oil. Cover with a 190-g (6½-oz) jar pesto sauce. Top with 150 g (5 oz) grated Cheddar cheese, 100 g (4 oz) sliced red onions and 225 g (8 oz) sliced tomatoes. Finish with a layer of thinly-sliced Mozzarella cheese (about 50 g/2 oz) and 1-2 tablespoons coarsely-chopped fresh basil leaves. Bake as above.

First Impressions

Some people behave as though there was an unwritten law
that states you must always serve a 'first course'.
That's rubbish.

It may suit you, or suit your guests, to just have a main
course followed by fruit and cheese, or a starter followed by
a pudding. That's why we've selected first courses that can be
juggled around.

They can create your first course impression for a three-
course dinner party or be adjusted to become a main feature
– it all depends on you.

Nanette

SARAH

Pumpkin Soup

This is wonderful as a first course before a traditional Thanksgiving feast.

SERVES 6

450 g (1 lb) fresh pumpkin, peeled and cut into small cubes

2 large potatoes, peeled and chopped

900 ml (1½ pints) chicken stock

750 ml (1¼ pints) milk

½ teaspoon ground nutmeg

½ teaspoon ground ginger

1 teaspoon salt

freshly ground black pepper

6 tablespoons soured cream

Boil the pumpkin in lightly-salted water until tender, about 45 minutes. Drain and set aside. Boil the potatoes in lightly-salted water until tender, about 15–20 minutes. Drain and set aside.

Place the pumpkin, potatoes and about half of the chicken stock in a blender or food processor and purée until smooth.

Place in a large saucepan and add the remaining stock, milk, nutmeg, ginger and salt and pepper to taste, mixing well. Bring to the boil, reduce the heat and simmer for 5 minutes. Serve hot in soup bowls topped with a spoonful of soured cream.

EMMA

Vegetable Soup with Rice

SERVES 4

3 tablespoons sunflower oil

1 onion, peeled and chopped

4 leeks, washed and thinly sliced

4 large carrots, peeled and grated

2 large potatoes, peeled and cubed

50 g (2 oz) long-grain rice

1.2 litres (2 pints) chicken stock

salt

freshly ground black pepper

Heat the oil in a large pan, add the onion and leeks and sauté until softened and translucent. Add the grated carrots and cook for about 3 minutes.

Stir in the potatoes, rice, stock and salt and pepper, mixing well. Bring to the boil, reduce the heat and simmer for about 2 hours, or until the vegetables and rice are very tender. Cool slightly.

Purée in a blender or food processor until smooth. Return to the pan and reheat until hot. Serve hot with garlic bread or topped with bread croûtons.

First Impressions

NANETTE

Chilled Pink Soup

This soup is lovely just as it is. I serve it with chunks of black bread. You can pass around a bowl of croûtons and finely-chopped spring onions.

SERVES 6

15 g (½ oz) butter
2 onions, peeled and chopped
2 carrots, peeled and grated
6 (medium) cooked beetroot, skinned and grated
1.8 litres (3 pints) chicken stock
2 teaspoons sugar
juice of 1 lemon
salt
freshly ground black pepper
1 teaspoon creamed horseradish
450 ml (¾ pint) soured cream
chopped fresh dill

Melt the butter in a large pan. Add the onions and carrots and cook for about 10 minutes but don't let them brown. Add the beetroot, stock and sugar and simmer for 30 minutes.

Mix in the lemon juice, salt and pepper to taste and horseradish. Cool then purée in a blender or food processor until smooth. Chill thoroughly.

Stir the soured cream into the soup and ladle into chilled soup bowls. Serve sprinkled with chopped fresh dill.

SARAH

Red Pepper Soup

When my husband was appearing in Noel Coward's *Tonight at 8.30*, one of the acts was called 'Red Peppers'. For a first night party I made this, but it's so good that I've been cooking it ever since. You can serve it hot or cold.

SERVES 6

15 g (½ oz) butter
1 tablespoon olive oil
6 medium red peppers, cored, seeded and cut into pieces
1 large onion, peeled and cut into pieces
1 medium potato, peeled and cut into pieces
1 clove of garlic, peeled and crushed
1.8 litres (3 pints) chicken stock
1 bay leaf
salt
freshly ground black pepper
250 ml (8 fl oz) buttermilk or single cream

Heat together the butter and oil in a large pan. Add the peppers, onion, potato and garlic. Cover and cook, over a moderate heat, until tender but not brown, stirring whenever you think about it.

Add the chicken stock, bay leaf and salt and pepper. Bring to the boil, reduce the heat, cover and simmer for 45–50 minutes, or until all the vegetables are tender. Remove and discard the bay leaf.

Purée in a blender or food processor until smooth. Stir in the buttermilk or single cream and adjust the seasoning if necessary. Serve hot or chilled.

RED PEPPER SOUP

SARAH

Watercress Soup

Mummy used to make this a lot and now it's my favourite soup.

SERVES 4

50 g (2 oz) butter
450 g (1 lb) leeks, washed and sliced
450 g (1 lb) potatoes, peeled and chopped
900 ml (1½ pints) chicken or vegetable stock
salt
freshly ground black pepper
2 bunches of watercress, trimmed
150 ml (¼ pint) double cream

Melt the butter in a large pan. Add the leeks and potatoes and cook for about 5 minutes, stirring constantly. Add the stock and salt and pepper to taste and bring to the boil. Reduce the heat, cover and simmer for 15 minutes, or until the vegetables are tender. Add the watercress and simmer for a further 5–7 minutes.

Purée the soup in a blender or food processor until smooth. To serve hot, return the soup to the pan and heat through gently. Stir in the cream just before serving. To serve cold, allow to cool then chill thoroughly. Swirl the cream into the chilled soup before serving.

NANETTE: When I make this soup I don't cook the watercress – I just cook the vegetables, as in Sarah's recipe, then purée with the raw watercress. I think it gives a slightly sharper taste.

NANETTE

Chilled Carrot and Pear Soup

SERVES 4

25 g (1 oz) butter
450 g (1 lb) carrots, peeled and sliced
6 spring onions, trimmed and thinly sliced
2 ripe pears, peeled, cored and chopped
450 ml (¾ pint) chicken stock
grated rind and juice of 1 orange
salt
freshly ground black pepper
150 ml (¼ pint) double cream
chopped fresh mint

Melt the butter in a large pan. Add the carrots and spring onions and cook for about 5 minutes but do not allow to brown. Stir in the pears and cook for another 5 minutes. Add the chicken stock, orange rind, orange juice and salt and pepper. Bring to the boil, reduce the heat, cover and simmer until the carrots are tender. Cool slightly.

Purée in a blender or food processor. Chill thoroughly. Just before serving stir the cream into the chilled soup. Serve sprinkled with the chopped mint.

NANETTE

Chilled Tomato Soup

Tomato soup always sounds very ordinary but when it's home-made it tastes anything but.

SERVES 4

1.25 kg (2½ lb) very ripe tomatoes, skinned
2 tablespoons cornflour
1 tablespoon sugar
1 teaspoon onion juice
grated rind and juice of 1 lemon
salt
freshly ground black pepper
150 ml (¼ pint) double cream
chopped fresh basil

Purée the tomatoes in a blender or food processor then sieve to remove any pips (you should have about 600 ml/1 pint purée). Mix the cornflour with a little of the purée then stir into the remainder. Heat gently, stirring until slightly thickened.

Remove from the heat, stir in the sugar, onion juice, lemon rind, lemon juice and salt and pepper to taste. Cool, cover and chill thoroughly.

Just before serving, beat the cream into the chilled tomato mixture. Taste and adjust the seasoning if necessary. Serve in chilled bowls sprinkled with some chopped fresh basil.

NANETTE

Pepper and Anchovy Hors d'Oeuvres

This is an unusual starter that tastes much better than it reads. I first had it in a little Italian restaurant and they kindly let me have the recipe.

SERVES 4

2 red peppers, cored, seeded and sliced
2 green peppers, cored, seeded and sliced
few drops of vinegar
50 g (2 oz) can anchovies, drained
15 g (½ oz) butter
4 teaspoons walnut oil
150 ml (¼ pint) double cream

Cook the peppers in boiling water with a few drops of vinegar, until just tender. Drain and reserve.

Purée the anchovies or pound to a smooth paste with a pestle and mortar. Heat the butter and oil in a pan, add the anchovies and cook gently for 1 minute over a low heat. Add the cream and stir until thickened but don't let it boil.

Place the peppers in a heated serving dish. Pour over the anchovy cream to coat then serve at once with chunks of toasted wholemeal bread.

EMMA

Peanut Dip with Crudités

For parties, a dinner party starter or even a snack.

SERVES 4

4 tablespoons peanut butter
50 g (2 oz) butter, melted
1 tablespoon soured cream
1 tablespoon mayonnaise
100 g (4 oz) cream or curd cheese
freshly ground black pepper

Purée the peanut butter, butter, soured cream, mayonnaise and cheese in a blender or food processor until smooth. Season to taste with pepper and spoon into a small serving bowl.

Chill before serving the dip surrounded with raw vegetables – for example, carrot sticks, whole mushrooms, pepper strips, cauliflower florets and celery chunks.

NANETTE

Stuffed Chicory Leaves

SERVES 4–6

2 heads of chicory
1 bunch of radishes, trimmed and very finely chopped
175 g (6 oz) cooked ham, finely chopped
2 tablespoons mayonnaise or soured cream
a small handful of cashew nuts, chopped

Separate the chicory heads into single leaves. Rinse and dry.

Mix the radishes with the ham, mayonnaise or soured cream and cashew nuts. Spoon a little along each chicory leaf. Arrange on a large plate to serve with drinks.

If you're looking for something easy but stylish to serve with drinks, then try this delicious appetiser that I first tasted at a party in Hollywood. Bake scrubbed and pricked tiny potatoes in their skins until tender. When cooked, scoop out a small amount of the cooked potato and fill with a spoonful of soured cream. Top with caviar.

Nanette

STUFFED CHICORY LEAVES

NANETTE

Watercress Mousse

SERVES 4–6

15 g (½ oz) powdered gelatine
3 tablespoons cold water
150 ml (¼ pint) boiling chicken stock
175 g (6 oz) cream cheese
1 teaspoon onion juice
2 tablespoons tarragon wine vinegar
1 tablespoon castor sugar
pinch of ground coriander
salt
freshly ground black pepper
2 large bunches of watercress, trimmed and finely chopped
150 ml (¼ pint) double cream

Sprinkle the gelatine over the cold water and leave until spongy. Add the boiling chicken stock and stir well to dissolve.

Place the cream cheese in a bowl and beat to soften. Gradually add the gelatine mixture, stirring well. Add the onion juice, vinegar, sugar, coriander and salt and pepper, mixing well. Fold in the watercress. Chill for about 10 minutes or until just beginning to set.

Meanwhile, whip the cream until it stands in soft peaks. Fold into the mousse mixture. Pour into a small, lightly-oiled ring mould or 600-ml (1-pint) decorative mould and chill to set.

Serve plain, with prawns or with extra watercress tossed in a light vinaigrette dressing. Alternatively, scoop and serve in the centre of halved and stoned avocados.

NANETTE

Tuna Mousse

I sometimes make this mousse in individual moulds – I turn them out then gently wrap in a slice of smoked salmon.

SERVES 6–8

439 g (15½ oz) can tuna, drained
300 ml (½ pint) mayonnaise
1 heaped dessertspoon creamed horseradish
300 ml (½ pint) double cream, whipped
2 tablespoons chopped fresh parsley
1 tablespoon chopped fresh dill
1 tablespoon lemon juice
salt
freshly ground black pepper
15 g (½ oz) powdered gelatine
4 tablespoons water
2 egg whites
¼ cucumber, sliced
chopped fresh dill

Purée the tuna, 2 tablespoons of the mayonnaise and the horseradish in a blender or food processor until smooth. Add the cream, remaining mayonnaise, parsley, dill, lemon juice and salt and pepper to taste, mixing well.

Dissolve the gelatine in the water and stir into the tuna mixture. Whisk the egg whites until they stand in stiff peaks. Fold into the tuna mixture. Pour into a lightly-oiled 1.25-litre (2¼-pint) ring mould, cover and chill until set – about 2 hours.

To serve, dip briefly into hot water and invert onto a serving plate. Serve surrounded with cucumber slices and sprinkled with chopped fresh dill.

EMMA: I occasionally make this as a main course and fill the centre of the ring with shrimps.

EMMA

Smoked Fish Pâté

This is so easy to make. It's delicious served as a starter with brown toast, or as a dip with raw carrot and celery strips.

SERVES 4–6

4 smoked mackerel fillets, skinned and boned

100 g (4 oz) cream cheese

2 tablespoons horseradish relish

juice of 1 lemon (or even more if you like a lemony taste)

50 g (2 oz) butter, melted

150 ml (¼ pint) double cream

freshly ground black pepper

Put everything in a blender or food processor and purée until smooth.

Add pepper to taste, mixing well. Spoon into a serving dish and chill.

SARAH: I make this as well – but I use smoked trout instead of mackerel.

Herbed Pitta Bread is a tasty extra to serve with drinks, soups, salads, mousses and pâtés. Open out slices of pitta bread, spread with butter and sprinkle with chopped fresh herbs. Sprinkle lightly with sea salt and place on a baking tray. Bake in a preheated oven, 200°C/400°F (gas mark 6), for about 10 minutes until crisp and golden. Pile into a basket and serve.

Emma

NANETTE

Mediterranean Prawns with Avocado

This avocado dip will discolour slightly after standing for a couple of hours so don't make too far in advance of eating.

SERVES 4

24 Mediterranean prawns

1 ripe avocado, halved and stoned

100 g (4 oz) cream cheese

1 tablespoon mayonnaise

juice of 1 lemon

salt

freshly ground black pepper

2 tablespoons chopped fresh chives

Remove the heads and shells from the prawns and discard, just leaving the tails intact. Arrange the prawns hanging over the edge of a glass serving bowl, half-filled with crushed ice, with the tails on the outside of the dish.

Place the avocado, cheese, mayonnaise, lemon juice and salt and pepper in a blender or food processor and purée until smooth. Pour into a small dish that will sit firmly on top of the crushed ice. Sprinkle or stir in the chives just before serving.

SARAH

Pears Filled with Smoked Chicken

SERVES 4

2 large ripe dessert pears, peeled, halved and cored

1 tablespoon lemon juice

100 g (4 oz) cream cheese

2 tablespoons soured cream

2 tablespoons crushed roasted hazelnuts

100 g (4 oz) smoked chicken, finely chopped

salt

freshly ground black pepper

a selection of salad leaves (for example, frisée and lambs' lettuce)

Dressing:

2 tablespoons hazelnut oil

2 teaspoons wine vinegar

pinch of finely-grated lemon rind

Poach the pears in boiling water with the lemon juice until barely tender. Drain and place in iced water to cool for about 2 minutes. Drain on absorbent paper.

Beat the cream cheese with the soured cream, hazelnuts, chicken and salt and pepper. Pile the mixture into the pear halves. Place each pear half on an individual salad leaf-lined plate.

To make the dressing, beat the oil with the vinegar, lemon rind and salt and pepper to taste. Drizzle over the salad leaves just before serving.

NANETTE: You can use raw pears for this dish but you would have to serve them almost immediately so that they don't discolour – brushing with a little lemon juice helps to prevent this.

First Impressions

PEARS FILLED WITH SMOKED CHICKEN

SARAH

Chicken Saté

This is good to serve with drinks before dinner.

SERVES 4–6

700 g (1½ lb) boneless chicken breasts, skinned
3 tablespoons sunflower oil
3 tablespoons soy sauce
1 clove of garlic, peeled and crushed
1½ teaspoons garam masala
2 teaspoons caster sugar

Saté Sauce:

2 tablespoons sunflower oil
100 g (4 oz) ground salted peanuts
1 onion, peeled and minced
1 clove of garlic, peeled and crushed
1 teaspoon chilli powder
1 teaspoon ground coriander
pinch of ground cumin
300 ml (½ pint) coconut milk or light chicken stock
2 tablespoons light brown sugar
1 tablespoon soy sauce
1 tablespoon lemon juice

Cut the meat into bite-sized cubes and place in a bowl. Mix the oil with the soy sauce, garlic, garam masala and sugar. Pour over the chicken and move around gently to coat. Cover and leave to marinate in a cool place for 4–6 hours.

To make the sauce, heat the oil in a pan. Add the ground peanuts, onion, garlic, chilli powder, coriander and cumin and sauté gently for 2 minutes. Add the coconut milk or stock, sugar, soy sauce and lemon juice. Bring to the boil, reduce the heat and simmer for 10 minutes, or until thick and creamy. Cool.

Thread the chicken onto small wooden skewers (soaked in water for about 30 minutes before using) and brush with some of the peanut sauce. Cook under a preheated hot grill for about 6–8 minutes, turning frequently and basting with the sauce from time to time.

Serve hot with any of the remaining saté sauce spooned over.

First Impressions

NANETTE

Grapefruit Sorbet

Bryan once worked with a producer who took Sarah out to lunch for a treat (she was about six at the time). He insisted on starting the meal with ice cream – saying 'Doesn't everybody?'. Naturally he was one of Sarah's favourite people after that. This is a good children's starter.

SERVES 4

300 ml (½ pint) water
150 g (5 oz) sugar
150 ml (¼ pint) fresh grapefruit juice (pink grapefruit is nice)
1 egg white

Place the water and sugar in a heavy-based pan. Heat slowly to dissolve the sugar then boil for about 6 minutes. Add the grapefruit juice (strained if necessary), mixing well, and leave to cool.

Pour into a shallow freezer tray and freeze until mushy (about 1 hour).

Transfer the grapefruit mixture to a bowl and whisk until smooth. Whisk the egg white until it stands in stiff peaks. Fold into the grapefruit mixture. Return to the freezer tray, cover, seal and freeze until firm or spoon into scooped-out orange or grapefruit shells and freeze until firm.

About 30 minutes before serving, put the sorbet in the refrigerator to soften. Spoon into chilled glasses or set the fruit shells on individual serving plates. Serve at once.

EMMA

Tomato Sorbet

SERVES 4–6

**4 very large ripe tomatoes, skinned
2 drops of Tabasco or 2 teaspoons
Worcestershire sauce
juice of ½ lemon
salt
freshly ground black pepper
1 egg white
fresh mint sprigs
1 lemon, sliced**

Cut the tomatoes in half and squeeze over a fine sieve to remove the seeds, keeping the strained juice. Chop the tomatoes and put in a blender or food processor with the tomato juice, Tabasco or Worcestershire sauce, lemon juice and salt and pepper. Purée until smooth, pour into a shallow freezer tray and freeze until mushy (about 1 hour).

Whirl in the blender or food processor or beat with a whisk until smooth. Whisk the egg white until it stands in stiff peaks. Fold into the tomato mixture. Return to the freezer tray, cover, seal and freeze until firm.

About 30 minutes before serving, remove the sorbet from the freezer to the refrigerator to soften. Spoon into chilled wine glasses and serve garnished with fresh mint and lemon slices. Serve at once.

EMMA

Cucumber and Grape Jelly

The perfect starter for hot summer days.

SERVES 4–6

**125 g (4¾ oz) packet lime-flavoured jelly
1 small cucumber, peeled and thinly sliced
salt
freshly ground white pepper
100 g (4 oz) seedless white grapes, halved
lemon slices
watercress sprigs**

Dissolve the jelly in hot water to make up to 450 ml (¾ pint) and let it cool until syrupy but not set.

Put the cucumber slices between sheets of absorbent paper and press them to remove excess water.

Season the jelly with salt and pepper. Add the cucumber and grapes and mix. Spoon into a serving dish or decorative mould and chill to set (preferably overnight or for 4–6 hours).

Serve with lemon slices and watercress.

R aw mangetout and lightly-steamed French beans look and taste good arranged around this quick and easy dip: Purée a small packet of Boursin cheese with 100 g (4 oz) cream cheese and a small ripe pear in a blender or food processor until smooth.

Emma

First Impressions

EMMA

Mushroom and Peanut Puffs

This is a spicy starter that I acquired from a friend of mine, Andrew. I have made these for lots of my dinner parties.

SERVES 4

50 g (2 oz) butter
225 g (8 oz) button mushrooms, wiped and halved if large
2 cloves of garlic, peeled and crushed
2 tablespoons smooth peanut butter
2 tablespoons soy sauce
¼ teaspoon chilli powder
salt
freshly ground black pepper
250 g (8¾ oz) packet frozen puff pastry, thawed
beaten egg to glaze
250 ml (8 fl oz) dry white wine
fresh parsley

Melt the butter in a pan. Add the mushrooms and garlic and sauté until just softened. Add the peanut butter, soy sauce, chilli powder and salt and pepper to taste, mixing well. Simmer gently until the cooking juices are reduced.

Roll out the pastry and cut into eight 7.5-cm (3-inch) circles. Place on a dampened baking sheet and glaze with beaten egg. Bake in a preheated oven, 220°C/427°F (gas mark 7), for 8–10 minutes, or until well-risen, golden and crisp.

Place a circle of pastry on each of four individual serving plates. Stir the wine into the mushroom mixture and spoon over the pastry rounds. Top with a second pastry round and decorate with parsley.

EMMA

Pasta with Salami and Olives in Tomato Sauce

SERVES 6

1 tablespoon olive oil
350 g (12 oz) mixed colour pasta twists
2 tablespoons sunflower oil
½ onion, peeled and finely chopped
425 g (15 oz) can chopped tomatoes and 227 g (8 oz) can chopped tomatoes
1 beef stock cube dissolved in 2 tablespoons hot water
1 teaspoon cornflour
300 ml (½ pint) single cream
8 slices salami, cut into thin strips
salt
freshly ground black pepper
10 black olives
freshly-grated Parmesan cheese (optional)

Bring a large pan of water to the boil and add the olive oil and the pasta. Boil briskly, uncovered, for about 8–10 mintues (or according to the packet instructions), until the pasta is cooked *al dente*. Drain thoroughly and keep warm.

Meanwhile, heat the oil in a large pan. Add the onion and sauté until softened. Stir in the tomatoes and cook until hot. Pour in the beef stock and cornflour dissolved in a little cold water. Simmer over a gentle heat for about 15 minutes, stirring occasionally.

Add the cream to the tomato mixture with the salami and salt and pepper to taste. Cook over a very gentle heat until bubbles just appear on the surface of the sauce.

Place the pasta in a shallow ovenproof dish and pour over the sauce, mixing well. Sprinkle with the olives and a little freshly-grated Parmesan cheese, if used. Bake in a preheated oven, 200°C/400°F (gas mark 6), for 10 minutes.

Serve hot with a tomato and cucumber salad tossed in vinaigrette dressing.

PASTA WITH SALAMI AND OLIVES IN TOMATO SAUCE

SARAH

Watercress and Walnut Salad with Blue Cheese Vinaigrette

This is a first course that you can make in a flash – the secret is in the dressing, so make sure you use the finest ingredients and don't substitute. It's a great way of cheering up left-over ham or chicken.

SERVES 4–6

1 head Iceberg lettuce, coarsely chopped
1 small head Cos or Romaine lettuce, coarsely chopped
2 large bunches of watercress, trimmed
75 g (3 oz) fresh shelled young baby peas
2 green dessert apples, cored and thinly sliced
75 g (3 oz) walnut halves, lightly roasted and coarsely broken
Dressing:
2 tablespoons finely-chopped or minced shallots
2 tablespoons cider vinegar
2 tablespoons lemon juice
¾ teaspoon cracked black pepper
½ teaspoon caster sugar
½ teaspoon salt
150 ml (¼ pint) walnut oil
75 g (3 oz) blue cheese, crumbled

To make the dressing, mix the shallots with the vinegar, lemon juice, pepper, sugar and salt. Gradually whisk in the oil and stir in the blue cheese. Cover and leave for 1 hour.

Put all the salad ingredients in a large serving bowl.

Pour the dressing over the salad and toss gently.

First Impressions

NANETTE

Pear and Stilton Salad

SERVES 4

3 tablespoons walnut oil
1 tablespoon wine vinegar
½ teaspoon Dijon mustard
salt
freshly ground black pepper
2 bunches of watercress, trimmed
4 ripe pears, peeled, cored and thinly sliced
175 g (6 oz) Stilton cheese, crumbled
4 tablespoons chopped walnuts

Beat the oil with the vinegar, mustard and salt and pepper to taste. Arrange the watercress in the centre of four dinner plates then arrange the pears attractively on top. Pour the dressing over the pears. Sprinkle with the cheese and walnuts.

Serve with oatmeal crackers.

EMMA

Cucumber and Tomato Minted Salad

This is a fresh-tasting salad to serve as a starter or as a side dish with pasta.

SERVES 4

½ cucumber, cut into thin strips
2 small tomatoes, sliced
4 carrots, peeled and grated
Dressing:
2 tablespoons sunflower oil
3 tablespoons mint sauce
1 teaspoon French mustard
1 teaspoon clear honey
salt
freshly ground black pepper

Put the cucumber in a serving bowl with the tomatoes and carrots. To make the dressing, beat the oil with the mint sauce, mustard, honey and salt and pepper to taste. Pour over the salad and toss. Cover and chill for about 1 hour before serving.

Short on time, then chop watermelon into cubes and place in chilled glasses. Sprinkle with vodka and serve. Sounds odd but tastes sensational!

Nanette

NANETTE

Cheese and Herb Soufflés

People are always impressed by soufflés – and yet they really couldn't be easier to make. Just make sure everyone has been seated a few minutes before you take them out of the oven.

SERVES 4

25 g (1 oz) butter
25 g (1 oz) plain flour
300 ml (½ pint) milk
4 eggs, separated
1 egg white
50 g (2 oz) Cheddar cheese, grated
50 g (2 oz) freshly-grated Parmesan cheese
salt
freshly ground black pepper
3 tablespoons chopped fresh herbs

Prepare 4 small soufflé or ovenproof soup bowls by buttering lightly then coating with a little Parmesan cheese or breadcrumbs.

Melt the butter in a pan. Add the flour and cook for 1 minute. Gradually add the milk, bring to the boil, stirring until smooth and thickened. Remove from the heat and stir in the egg yolks, one at a time, mixing well. Add the cheeses, salt and pepper and the herbs.

Whisk the egg whites until they stand in stiff peaks. Stir 1 tablespoon into the cheese mixture then fold in the remainder. Divide between the prepared bowls and bake in a preheated oven, 180°C/350°F (gas mark 4), for about 20 minutes, or until puffed-up and pale brown on top (keep your eyes on them).

To serve, place each soufflé on a napkin in the centre of a large dinner plate. Serve at once, of course.

* Fresh Parmesan cheese is so much nicer than the ready-grated sort.

CHEESE AND HERB SOUFFLÉS

First Impressions

SARAH

Fried Brie with Raspberry Purée

Sounds odd – tastes great.

SERVES 4

about a 350–400 g (12–14 oz) wedge Brie cheese, not too ripe
50 g (2 oz) plain wholewheat flour
2 eggs, beaten
175 g (6 oz) wholewheat breadcrumbs
25 g (1 oz) flaked almonds, coarsely chopped
450 g (1 lb) frozen raspberries
6 tablespoons water
50 g (2 oz) sugar
oil for deep frying

Remove the rind from the Brie and cut into 12 pieces about the size of a walnut. Dust with the flour, dip in the beaten egg and roll in the breadcrumbs and almonds to coat. Chill for at least 2 hours for the coating to become firm before cooking.

Meanwhile, to make the sauce, place the raspberries, water and sugar in a heavy-based pan and cook until pulpy, about 10 minutes. Cool slightly then sieve to remove the seeds.

Heat the oil in a deep-fat fryer or pan to about 190°C/375°F, or until a cube of bread will brown. Add the Brie pieces and deep-fry until crisp and golden. Drain well on absorbent paper.

Reheat the raspberry purée until hot. Place the Brie balls on a warmed serving plate and surround with the warm raspberry purée. They are delicious with French or other crisp, interesting bread.

EMMA

Avocados Baked with Brie

This is quick and easy – that's why I like it.

SERVES 4

2 avocados, halved and stoned
1 tablespoon lemon juice
about 175 (6 oz) Brie, thinly sliced

Brush the cut surface of each avocado with the lemon juice. Fill the hollows with sliced Brie.
 Cook under a preheated hot grill until the Brie is bubbly. Serve at once.

NANETTE

Bananas with Prosciutto

Everyone has melon, pear or fig with prosciutto – but banana is also delicious.

SERVES 4

4 large bananas
1 tablespoon lemon juice
freshly ground black pepper
12 thin slices prosciutto crudo or Parma ham
fresh parsley sprigs

Brush the bananas with the lemon juice. Season generously with freshly ground black pepper. Wrap in the slices of ham and serve on individual serving plates. Garnish with sprigs of parsley.

Dinner Parties

If you are giving a dinner party the menu usually slots into place once you have decided upon the main course.

You can make the principal course your star turn and forget about starters or puddings. Serve something with drinks before dinner and offer fruit and cheese at the end.

Whichever way you choose to organise your dinners, here are some of our collective ideas.

Nanette

NANETTE

Striped Fish Terrine

SERVES 4

225 g (8 oz) haddock fillets, skinned
50 g (2 oz) fresh white breadcrumbs
1 tablespoon milk
2 eggs, beaten
1 tablespoon fromage frais
1 tablespoon double cream
2 tablespoons chopped fresh parsley
1 tablespoon chopped fresh chives
pinch of ground nutmeg
pinch of cayenne pepper
salt
freshly ground black pepper
450 g (1 lb) spinach leaves
3–4 scallops (depending upon size)

Put the haddock fillets in a blender or food processor and process until finely chopped. Soak the breadcrumbs in the milk, add to the fish with the eggs, fromage frais, cream, parsley, chives, nutmeg, cayenne pepper and salt and pepper. Purée until smooth.

Trim, sort and wash the spinach leaves. Place in a pan with just the water clinging to the leaves. Cook until limp, squeeze to remove any excess water then chop very finely. Stir in the fish mixture, mixing well.

Trim and discard any black vein from the scallops. Separate the white flesh from the coral. Thinly slice the white flesh horizontally.

Line a 900-ml (1½-pint) terrine with greased foil. Place half of the fish mixture in the base of the terrine and cover with the white scallop flesh and corals, pressing down firmly. Top with the remaining fish mixture, cover tightly with greased foil and place in a *bain-marie* or roasting pan half-filled with boiling water. Cook in a preheated oven, 180°C/350°F (gas mark 4), for 1 hour.

Remove the terrine from the *bain-marie* and leave to cool. Unmould onto a serving plate, cover and chill thoroughly. It is very good with home-made tomato sauce or home-made mayonnaise flavoured sharply with lemon.

EMMA	NANETTE

Lemon Cod

This fish dish is easy on the pocket and the waistline.

SERVES 4

4 cod steaks
juice of 2 lemons
2 tablespoons green or pink peppercorns
50 g (2 oz) butter
fresh dill
freshly ground black pepper

Place each cod steak on a piece of foil large enough to enclose the fish. Squeeze over the lemon juice and peppercorns. Dot with the butter and top with a few sprigs of fresh dill and pepper to taste. Fold and secure into a parcel shape.

Bake in a preheated oven, 180°C/350°F (gas mark 4), for 30 minutes, or until the fish is cooked and flakes easily with a fork. Serve hot in the foil envelopes with jacket-baked potatoes.

When the children lived at home I had an enormous long table because there always seemed to be so many of us. I now have a fairly large round table, which I love. It will seat ten (just), eight (comfortably) or four (spaciously). I also have really comfortable wicker dining chairs, with arms and cushions. Don't you hate sitting on hard, uncomfortable chairs at a dinner party – I do.

Nanette

Lemon Sole Stuffed with Smoked Salmon and Spinach

This is a very special, very simple, dinner party dish to serve two people, but it's easy to prepare for many more.

SERVES 2

1 large lemon sole
100 g (4 oz) cooked chopped spinach
2 tablespoons cream cheese
pinch of ground nutmeg
salt
freshly ground black pepper
2 very thin slices smoked salmon
juice of 1 lemon
40 g (1½ oz) butter, melted
fresh tarragon leaves

Ask the fishmonger to skin and fillet the sole to give you two fillets. Mix the spinach with the cheese, nutmeg and salt and pepper. Place a slice of smoked salmon on each lemon sole fillet. Divide the stuffing evenly and spread over the fish. Roll the fillet up loosely to enclose the filling and secure with wooden cocktail sticks.

Place in a buttered ovenproof dish and squeeze over the lemon juice. Brush with the melted butter and scatter over a few fresh tarragon leaves. Cook in a preheated oven, 180°C/350°F (gas mark 4), for 15 minutes.

Serve hot with tiny new potatoes and mangetout.

LEMON SOLE STUFFED WITH SMOKED SALMON AND SPINACH

SARAH

Gingered Salmon en Croûte

SERVES 8

1.25 kg (2½ lb) salmon tailpiece
100 g (4oz) butter
3 tablespoons raisins
3 tablespoons blanched almonds, coarsely chopped
4 pieces preserved ginger, chopped
10 cooked asparagus spears
salt
freshly ground black pepper
450 g (1 lb) shortcrust pastry
beaten egg to glaze
Herb and Lemon Sauce:
50 g (2 oz) butter
2 shallots, peeled and finely chopped
1 teaspoon finely-chopped fresh chervil
1 teaspoon finely-chopped fresh tarragon
1 teaspoon finely-chopped fresh parsley
1 teaspoon plain flour
300 ml (½ pint) single cream
1 teaspoon Dijon mustard
2 egg yolks
juice of 1 lemon

Ask the fishmonger to skin and bone the salmon into two fillets. Mix the butter with the raisins, almonds and ginger. Spread half of this filling over one of the salmon fillets and top with the asparagus spears. Season generously with salt and pepper. Cover with the second fish fillet and remaining butter mixture.

Roll out the pastry thinly and cut out two long oval shapes. Place the fish sandwich on top of one of the pastry pieces, set on a lightly-greased baking tray. Cover with the second pastry piece and press the edges together firmly to seal. Trim and flute or crimp the edges attractively. Roll out the pastry trimmings and cut into small fish shapes. Glaze the pastry with beaten egg, place the decorative fish shapes in position and glaze again. Make a few deep slashes in the top of the pastry crust

to allow any steam to escape.

Bake in a preheated oven, 220°C/425°F (gas mark 7), for 30–35 minutes, until the fish is cooked and the pastry is crisp and golden.

Meanwhile, to make the sauce, melt the butter in a pan. Add the shallots, chervil, tarragon and parsley and cook until softened. Stir in the flour and then all but 2 tablespoons of the cream. Add the mustard and salt and pepper to taste. Simmer gently for 10 minutes. Mix the egg yolks with the reserved cream and stir into the sauce. Cook over a gentle heat until the sauce thickens – don't allow to boil. Add the lemon juice just before serving.

To serve, transfer the salmon to a warmed serving plate, surround with a selection of cooked vegetables. Serve with the hot Herb and Lemon Sauce.

SARAH

Fettucine with Smoked Salmon and Fresh Peas

SERVES 6

3 tablespoons olive oil

700 g (1½ lb) fettucine verdi

150 g (5 oz) shelled fresh peas or mangetout, trimmed

100 g (4 oz) thinly-sliced smoked salmon

600 ml (1 pint) double cream

1 tablespoon chopped shallot

2 tablespoons dry white wine

salt

freshly ground black pepper

Bring a large pan of water to the boil and add 1 tablespoon of the olive oil and the pasta. Boil briskly, uncovered, for 4–6 minutes (or according to the packet instructions), until the pasta is cooked *al dente*. Drain thoroughly, add the remaining olive oil and toss lightly to coat. Keep warm.

Meanwhile, blanch the peas or mangetout for 2 minutes, drain and plunge into iced water. Place half of the smoked salmon in a blender or food processor with 2 tablespoons of the double cream and the shallot. Purée until smooth. Cut the remaining smoked salmon into thin strips.

Place the wine in a heavy-based pan and bring to the boil. Add the remaining cream and cook, stirring constantly, until the mixture thickens and will coat the back of a spoon. Add the salmon purée, mixing well. Season to taste with salt and pepper.

Stir the peas or mangetout, salmon strips and hot sauce into the pasta. Toss lightly, spoon into a warmed serving dish and serve at once.

NANETTE

Herbed Lobster Parcels

Whenever we have dinner at Keith and Mary's house the food is always superb. This is Mary's recipe.

Serves 4

25 g (1 oz) butter
50 g (2 oz) fresh white breadcrumbs
700 g (1½ lb) cooked lobster, cut into bite-sized pieces
1 tablespoon chopped fresh chives
2 tablespoons chopped fresh parsley
1 tablespoon dry white wine
2 tablespoons mayonnaise
2 tablespoons natural yoghurt
salt
freshly ground black pepper
450 g (1 lb) frozen puff pastry, thawed
beaten egg to glaze

Melt the butter in a pan. Add the breadcrumbs and sauté gently until brown. Remove from the heat, add the lobster, chives, parsley, wine, mayonnaise, yoghurt and salt and pepper to taste, mixing well.

Roll out the pastry thinly to a 35-cm (14-inch) square, then cut into quarters.

Place a quarter of the lobster mixture in the centre of each pastry square. Brush the edges with beaten egg then bring each pastry corner to the centre and press firmly together to seal and enclose the filling. Place on a dampened baking tray and glaze with beaten egg.

Bake in a preheated oven, 200°C/400°F (gas mark 6), for 20–30 minutes, or until the pastry is well-risen, crisp and golden. Serve warm or cold.

EMMA: As an alternative, replace the cooked lobster with cooked chicken.

SARAH

Crabcakes

I secured this recipe from a favourite restaurant in Beverly Hills. It's the most popular dish on the menu.

MAKES 6

450 g (1 lb) crabmeat
juice of 1 lemon
25 g (1 oz) butter
75 g (3 oz) plain flour
10 tablespoons milk
½ teaspoon mustard powder
2 egg yolks
4 teaspoons capers, coarsely chopped
cayenne pepper
salt
freshly ground white pepper
1 egg
75 g (3 oz) fresh white breadcrumbs
25 g (1 oz) unsalted butter
2 tablespoons sunflower oil
lemon wedges
mayonnaise to serve

Mash the crabmeat with the lemon juice. Melt the butter in a pan. Add one-third of the flour and cook for 1 minute. Gradually add 6 table-spoons of the milk and bring to the boil, stirring constantly, until smooth and thickened. Remove from the heat, stir in the mustard, egg yolks, capers, cayenne pepper and salt and white pepper to taste, mixing well. Stir in the crabmeat mixture and mix. Cover and chill for at least 1 hour.

Divide and shape the crabmeat mixture into 6 patties. Coat in the remaining flour. Beat the egg with the remaining milk. Dip the patties into the milk mixture then in the breadcrumbs to coat. Chill thoroughly to firm for about 1 hour before cooking.

To cook, heat together the unsalted butter and the oil in a large frying pan. Add the crabcakes and sauté until golden and crisp on all sides. Drain on absorbent paper.

Serve hot with huge wedges of lemon and lashings of mayonnaise.

NANETTE

Pike and Caviar

My friend Veronica owns a superb restaurant in London – this is one of her inventions. It is often on the menu and always in demand.

SERVES 4

225 g (8 oz) filleted pike
300 ml (½ pint) double cream
2 eggs
2 egg yolks
salt
freshly ground white pepper
40 g (1½ oz) butter, melted
40 g (1½ oz) smoked salmon, cut into strips
fresh dill
Sauce:
150 ml (¼ pint) fish stock
1 tablespoon lemon juice
25 ml (1 fl oz) dry white wine
150 ml (¼ pint) double cream
50 g (2 oz) red or black caviar (or 'mock caviar')

Purée the pike in a blender or food processor until smooth. Pass through a fine sieve then return to the blender or food processor. Add the cream, eggs, egg yolks and salt and pepper. Purée until smooth.

Brush 4 moulds (about 8.5 cm/3½ inches high by 5 cm/2 inches in diameter) with the melted butter. Half-fill with the fish purée. Top with the smoked salmon. Sprinkle each with 1 teaspoon chopped fresh dill and cover with the remaining fish purée.

Cover with buttered foil and place in a *bain-marie* or roasting dish half-full of hot water.

Cook in a preheated oven, 220°C/425°F (gas mark 7), for 30 minutes, or until firm when lightly touched.

To make the sauce, put the stock, lemon juice and wine in a small pan. Reduce until syrupy. Add the cream and cook until thickened. Stir in some chopped fresh dill and the caviar.

To serve, spoon the sauce onto 4 warmed serving plates. Turn out the pike moulds onto the plates and top each with a feathery sprig of dill.

Serve at once.

PIKE AND CAVIAR

TABLE IDEAS

☐ Fill a large bowl (or basket) with apples and decorate with leaves.

☐ Place a single rose in a small vase in front of each guest.

☐ Fill a bowl or basket with lots of African violets left in their pots, then tie trailing purple ribbons around your candlesticks.

☐ Scoop out the insides of globe artichokes and place a night light in the centre of each.

☐ Angela puts unusual flowers in jam jars, then ties a napkin around like a collar.

☐ Try arranging a large basket of raw vegetables with herbs and flowers for the centre of the table – you can then eat your table centrepiece with a dip as a first course.

☐ Collect lots of large fir cones, pile into a basket, add sprigs of holly, pine cones and walnuts. Decorate with red velvet bows and you have a Christmas table centrepiece that even the children can make.

Nanette

EMMA

Rice in a Wok with Prawns and Vegetables

SERVES 4–6

350 g (12 oz) long-grain rice
1 small onion, peeled and chopped
1 vegetable or fish stock cube
2 tablespoons vegetable or sesame oil
275 g (10 oz) peeled prawns
4 sticks of celery, chopped
1 red pepper, cored, seeded and chopped
1 green pepper, cored, seeded and chopped

Cook the rice with the onion and stock cube in boiling water, according to the packet instructions, until tender. Drain thoroughly.

Heat the oil in a large frying pan or wok. Add the prawns, celery and peppers and stir-fry for 2 minutes.

Add the cooked rice mixture and toss to mix. Stir-fry for 1–2 minutes or until hot. Serve at once.

NANETTE

Simple Chicken with Mint

Quick, easy and delicious – the perfect summer evening dish.

SERVES 6

6 chicken breasts, skinned

chicken stock

Dressing:

3 tablespoons safflower oil

3 tablespoons walnut oil

2 tablespoons white wine vinegar

1½ teaspoons Dijon mustard

½ teaspoon sugar

salt

freshly ground black pepper

very large bunch of fresh mint, chopped

Poach the chicken breasts in sufficient chicken stock to cover until tender, about 10 minutes. Cover and leave to cool in the stock.

When cool, remove from the stock and slice into thin strips.

To make the dressing, beat the oils with the vinegar, mustard, sugar and salt and pepper. Stir in the mint and pour over the chicken. Cover and leave to marinate for 1 hour.

To serve, arrange the chicken strips in a fan shape on a serving dish. Serve with tiny new potatoes and a crisp salad.

SARAH: The chicken may be served on individual serving dishes – the chicken slices arranged to alternate with thin slices of avocado and strips of cucumber. Serve with hot granary bread.

SARAH

Glazed Tarragon Turkey

SERVES 4

4 small unboned turkey breasts
salt
freshly ground black pepper
25 g (1 oz) butter
2 tablespoons finely-chopped shallot
2 tablespoons finely-chopped fresh tarragon
6 tablespoons dry white wine
3 tablespoons water

Season the turkey with salt and pepper. Melt the butter in a large frying pan, add the turkey breasts, skin-side down, and sauté until golden, about 10 minutes. Turn over and cook, over a gentle heat, for 5 minutes more. Remove the turkey from the pan with a slotted spoon and set aside.

Add the shallot to the pan juices and cook until softened. Stir in the tarragon, wine and water. Return the turkey breasts to the pan, skin-side up. Cover and cook, over a low heat, for 15 minutes.

Remove the cover and continue to cook, adding a little more wine if necessary, for a further 5 minutes, basting the turkey frequently with the juices, until tender and evenly glazed. Serve with a green vegetable.

GLAZED TARRAGON TURKEY

EMMA

Chicken in Breadcrumbs

Serve these crunchy chicken breasts on a bed of watercress with a spoonful of chutney.

SERVES 4

4 boneless chicken breasts, skinned
25 g (1 oz) plain flour
2 eggs, beaten
50 g (2 oz) granary breadcrumbs
4 slices smoked ham
4 slices Mozzarella cheese
salt
freshly ground black pepper

Coat the chicken breasts in the flour. Dip into the beaten egg and coat in the breadcrumbs. Chill for about 20 minutes.

Place on a baking tray and cook in a preheated oven, 190°C/375°F (gas mark 5), for 30–40 minutes, or until the chicken is cooked (when pierced any juices will run clear). Remove from the oven, cover each chicken breast with a slice of ham and a slice of cheese. Season with salt and pepper, return to the oven and cook for a further 8–10 minutes, or until the cheese is bubbly and melted.

> **M**y dining room is lit by candlelight, a log fire and nothing else. I have a stone fireplace and on the mantlepiece I sometimes line up plants (just left in their clay pots). African violets, geraniums, white daisies or miniature cyclamen are some of my favourites. Between them I place scented candles – try it!
>
> *Nanette*

EMMA

Chicken Baked with Honey, Courgette and Tomato

This is very easy to make and has a light subtle flavour. It's great served with a mixed salad or baked potatoes topped with soured cream and chives.

SERVES 4

4 chicken breasts, skinned
25 g (1 oz) plain flour
3 tablespoons sunflower oil
½ small onion, peeled and finely chopped
1 clove of garlic, peeled and crushed
6 medium courgettes, chopped
400 g (14 oz) can chopped tomatoes
salt
freshly ground black pepper
2 tablespoons clear honey

Lightly coat the chicken breasts in the flour. Heat 2 tablespoons of the oil in a frying pan. Add the chicken breasts and sauté until browned on all sides. Remove from the pan and place in a flameproof casserole dish.

Heat the remaining oil in a pan. Add the onion, garlic and courgettes and cook, over a moderate heat, until the onion is softened. Add the tomatoes and salt and pepper to taste and stir around.

Spread the honey over the chicken breasts, then pour over the tomato mixture. Cover and bake in a preheated oven, 180°C/350°F (gas mark 4), for 40 minutes. Remove from the oven and cook, uncovered, under a preheated hot grill until crisp and golden, about 10 minutes. Serve at once.

SARAH

Basil-rolled Chicken Breasts

This is the perfect make-ahead cold chicken dish – the chicken rolls can be made the day before required; the sauce can be whipped up just before it's needed; and a green salad and crusty bread are all you need to go with it.

SERVES 4

4 boneless chicken breasts, skinned

225 g (8 oz) fresh white breadcrumbs, lightly toasted

½ onion, peeled and finely chopped

1 clove of garlic, peeled and crushed

40 g (1½ oz) chopped fresh herbs (for example, basil, thyme, rosemary, parsley, sage and marjoram)

2 eggs, beaten

salt

freshly ground black pepper

Basil and Orange Sauce:

6 tablespoons olive oil

4 tablespoons orange juice

2 tablespoons lemon juice

grated rind of ½ orange

1 clove of garlic, peeled and crushed

2 tablespoons chopped fresh basil

mayonnaise

Place the chicken breasts between sheets of greaseproof paper and beat until flat.

Mix the breadcrumbs with the onion, garlic, herbs, beaten egg and salt and pepper to taste. Spread the stuffing over the rough side of the chicken breasts and roll up to enclose. Secure with wooden cocktail sticks. Place, seam-side down, on a lightly-greased baking dish. Cover with greaseproof paper and bake in a preheated oven, 190°C/375°F (gas mark 5), for 20–30 minutes, or until the chicken is cooked. Allow to cool.

To make the sauce, mix the oil with the orange juice, lemon juice, orange rind, garlic and basil. Add sufficient mayonnaise to the mixture to make a sauce that resembles a runny hollandaise.

Cut the stuffed, cooked chicken breasts diagonally into thin slices. Arrange on a serving plate. Drizzle over the sauce to serve.

STIR-FRIED DUCK WITH GINGER

EMMA

Stir-fried Duck with Ginger

Because I'm rather short of kitchen space I find cooking in the wok ideal. I usually serve this with a stir-fried rice dish or with a selection of stir-fried crispy vegetables.

SERVES 4

3 tablespoons sunflower oil
2.5-cm (1-inch) piece root ginger, peeled
4 duck breasts, skinned and cut into strips
227 g (8 oz) can bamboo shoots, drained
227 g (8 oz) can waterchestnuts, drained and sliced
½ red pepper, cored, seeded and sliced
½ yellow pepper, cored, seeded and sliced
2 spring onions, trimmed and chopped
soy sauce
1 tablespoon dry sherry

Heat the oil in a wok or large frying pan. Add the ginger and cook for 1 minute. Remove it with a slotted spoon and reserve. Cut the ginger in half and chop one half finely (discard the remainder).

Add the duck strips to the very hot oil and stir-fry, tossing constantly, until just cooked. Add the bamboo shoots, waterchestnuts, peppers, spring onions, the chopped reserved ginger, soy sauce to taste and sherry. Stir-fry for 1–2 minutes until very hot. Serve at once.

S ince my flat is small and open-plan, I have to be organised when I entertain. I usually serve food in the pan it has been cooked in or arrange everything on one enormous plate. This also cuts down on washing-up.

Emma

NANETTE

Chicken, Walnut and Apricot Pie

You can get carried away decorating this dish with pastry shapes. You can cut out your guests' initials, hearts or leaves – or whatever takes your fancy.

SERVES 6

50 g (2 oz) butter
1 onion, peeled and chopped
100 g (4 oz) button mushrooms, wiped and sliced
50 g (2 oz) plain flour
300 ml (½ pint) chicken stock
150 ml (¼ pint) dry white wine
25 g (1 oz) ground walnuts
450 g (1 lb) cooked chicken, thinly sliced
50 g (2 oz) cooked dried apricots, thinly sliced
1 tablespoon chopped fresh parsley
salt
freshly ground black pepper
370 g (13 oz) packet frozen puff pastry, thawed
beaten egg to glaze
2 teaspoons sesame seeds

Melt the butter in a pan. Add the onion and sauté until soft. Add the mushrooms and cook briefly. Stir in the flour and cook for 1 minute. Gradually add the chicken stock and wine. Stir in the walnuts, bring to the boil, stir until lightly thickened. Remove from the heat, fold in the chicken, apricots, parsley and salt and pepper. Spoon into a 1.5-litre (2½-pint) pie dish.

Roll out the pastry to a round or oval about 2.5 cm (1 inch) larger than the dish. Cut a narrow strip from around the pastry and use to cover the dampened rim of the dish. Brush the pastry rim with water and cover with the pastry lid. Seal the edges firmly, trim and crimp attractively. Decorate with cut-out pastry shapes. Make a hole in the crust to allow any steam to escape. Glaze with beaten egg and sprinkle with the sesame seeds.

Bake in a preheated oven, 200°C/400°F (gas mark 6), for 25–30 minutes, or until the pastry is well-risen, cooked and golden brown.

EMMA

Chicken in Soured Cream with Red Peppers and Avocado

This is a good dish to prepare for larger, buffet-style dinner parties.

SERVES 4

6 boneless chicken breasts
chicken stock
1 red pepper, cored, seeded and sliced
150 ml (¼ pint) soured cream
2 tablespoons mayonnaise
2 tablespoons chopped fresh chives
salt
freshly ground black pepper
1 ripe avocado, peeled, stoned and sliced
lettuce leaves
cooked French beans in vinaigrette dressing

Poach the chicken breasts in sufficient chicken stock to cover until tender, about 10 minutes. Cover and leave to cool in the stock.

When cool, remove from the stock and slice into thin strips.

Mix the chicken with the pepper. Blend the soured cream with the mayonnaise, chives and salt and pepper to taste. Fold into the chicken mixture with the avocado.

Serve on a bed of lettuce with cooked French beans in vinaigrette dressing.

NANETTE

Turkey Filo Roll

Filo pastry is so useful and simple to use – just make sure you assemble it quickly so that it doesn't dry out.

SERVES 4–6

100 g (4 oz) butter
1 clove of garlic, peeled and crushed
1 onion, peeled and chopped
50 g (2 oz) celery, chopped
450 g (1 lb) cooked turkey, finely chopped
2 tablespoons chicken stock
25 g (1 oz) flaked almonds
2 tablespoons chopped fresh herbs (for example, rosemary, thyme and marjoram)
pinch of ground nutmeg
1 egg, beaten
12 sheets filo pastry

Melt 15 g (½ oz) of the butter in a pan. Add the garlic, onion and celery and sauté until softened. Add the turkey and stock and cook for 1 minute. Remove from the heat and stir in the almonds, herbs, nutmeg and beaten egg.

Stack the pastry neatly, brushing between each layer with the remaining melted butter. Spoon the turkey mixture over the final layer to within 2.5 cm (1 inch) of the edges. Roll up as you would for a Swiss roll. Place, seam-side down, on a greased baking tray. Brush with melted butter.

Bake in a preheated oven, 180°C/350°F (gas mark 4), for 30–40 minutes, or until the pastry is lightly browned and crisp. Serve cut into thick slices.

EMMA

Pasta with Dolcelatte Cheese and Bacon

This is one of my favourite dinner party dishes as it is incredibly easy to prepare, delicious (very fattening!) and most impressive. Serve it with a chicory and orange or tomato and onion salad.

SERVES 6

1 tablespoon olive oil
500 g (18 oz) dried pasta shells or bows
600 ml (1 pint) double cream
450 g (1 lb) Dolcelatte cheese, crumbled
225 g (8 oz) cooked smoked streaky bacon, crumbled or chopped
freshly ground black pepper
chopped fresh parsley

Bring a large pan of water to the boil and add the olive oil and pasta. Boil briskly, uncovered, for 10–12 minutes (or according to the packet instructions), until the pasta is cooked *al dente*. Drain thoroughly. Spoon into a warmed serving dish and keep warm.

Meanwhile, place the cream and cheese in the top of a double boiler and cook until the cheese melts (don't take your eyes off it!). Add the bacon and pepper to taste, stirring well to mix together.

Pour over the cooked pasta and toss gently to coat. Serve at once sprinkled with plenty of chopped fresh parsley.

Dining with a brilliant Italian director was a great thrill. We ate on her terrace, high up, which had amazing views over Rome, with plants winding and trailing everywhere.

The table was laid with a black cloth, white candles in glass containers filled with pink geraniums, white plates and Art Nouveau glasses with wine from her own vineyard. We sat in black painted wicker chairs with pink cushions, the air scented with jasmine.

The first course was a perfect spaghetti with tomato sauce. The main course *Veal Tonnata* and a green salad.

For dessert, a tray appeared with a large frosted glass bowl filled with scoops of unusual flavoured ice creams. The bowl was surrounded by ice cream cones, standing like soldiers, which she filled with the chosen ice cream and passed around.

To complete the meal, a white cake stand, piled high with fat black cherries. Then tiny cups of strong coffee.

Nanette

NANETTE

Lamb Chops with Stuffed Pears

I rarely eat red meat, but I have friends who do and this is always popular.

SERVES 4

8 lamb loin chops
salt
freshly ground black pepper
4 ripe pears, peeled, halved and cored
juice of ½ lemon
4 tablespoons mint jelly
4 tablespoons redcurrant jelly
fresh mint sprigs

I prefer to cook lamb chops on a sheet of foil on a baking tray in the oven. The timing obviously depends upon the size and thickness of the chops and your guests' preference for pink or well-done meat. I can't bear people who insist that meat has to be eaten with blood oozing out – but it's a matter of taste – yours. Bake the seasoned chops in a preheated oven, 190°C/375°F (gas mark 5), until cooked to your liking.

Meanwhile, brush the pears with the lemon juice to prevent them turning brown. Place, hollow-sides up, in a shallow ovenproof dish. Place a tablespoon of mint jelly into four pear halves and the redcurrant jelly into the remaining halves. Place in the oven for the last 5 minutes' cooking time to heat through.

Serve the cooked lamb chops with the stuffed pears, garnished with sprigs of fresh mint. Delicious with steamed mangetout.

EMMA

Bramley Crown of Lamb

SERVES 4–6

4 teaspoons sunflower oil
1 small onion, peeled and chopped
1 stick of celery, chopped
100 g (4 oz) carrots, peeled and chopped
25 g (1 oz) sultanas
450 g (1 lb) Bramley apples, peeled, cored and chopped
50 g (2 oz) cooked long-grain rice
2 tablespoons chopped fresh parsley
lemon juice
salt
freshly ground black pepper
1 crown roast of lamb (with a total of 14 cutlets)
apple wedges
watercress sprigs

Heat 3 teaspoons of the oil in a pan. Add the onion and celery and sauté until just soft. Add the carrots, sultanas and apples and cook for 3–5 minutes, keep stirring. Add the rice and parsley then sharpen with lemon juice. Season with salt and pepper.

Place the crown roast in a greased roasting tin and fill the centre with the stuffing mixture, pressing down firmly. Cover the stuffing and bone ends with foil to prevent charring. Brush with the remaining oil and roast in a preheated oven, 190°C/375°F (gas mark 5), for 1¼–2 hours, according to taste.

Serve hot decorated with apple wedges and watercress.

SARAH

Classic Beef Carbonnade

SERVES 4–6

50 g (2 oz) butter
1 large onion, peeled and finely chopped
1 kg (2 lb) chuck steak, cubed
1 clove of garlic, peeled and crushed
450 ml (¾ pint) stout
2 teaspoons French mustard
2 teaspoons brown sugar
2 teaspoons malt vinegar
1 bay leaf
pinch of dried thyme
salt
freshly ground black pepper
50 g (2 oz) fresh white breadcrumbs

Melt the butter in a pan. Add the onion and sauté until golden. Add the beef and cook until browned on all sides. Add the garlic, stout, mustard, sugar, vinegar, bay leaf, thyme and salt and pepper. Bring to the boil then transfer to a casserole dish.

Cover and cook in a preheated oven, 160°C/325°F (gas mark 3), for 2–2½ hours, or until the beef is tender.

Just before serving, stir in the breadcrumbs.

NANETTE

Bobotie

I was given this recipe when I was in Johannesburg. It's really a more interesting Shepherd's Pie.

SERVES 4

1 large slice of bread, crusts removed
300 ml (½ pint) milk
25 g (1 oz) butter
1 onion, peeled and finely chopped
1 sweet apple, peeled, cored and chopped
1½ teaspoons curry powder
1 tablespoon mango chutney
25 g (1 oz) flaked almonds
15 g (½ oz) seedless raisins
1 tablespoon lemon juice
450 g (1 lb) minced cooked lamb
salt
freshly ground black pepper
2 eggs, beaten
few lemon, orange, lime or bay leaves

Place the bread in a bowl, pour over the milk and leave to soak.

Melt the butter in a pan. Add the onion and apple and sauté until softened. Add the curry powder, mango chutney, almonds, raisins and lemon juice and cook for 2 minutes.

Squeeze the excess milk from the bread and reserve. Mix the soaked bread with the lamb and stir into the curried mixture. Season with salt and pepper. Spoon into a medium pie dish and bake in a preheated oven, 180°C/350°F (gas mark 4), for 15 minutes.

Meanwhile, mix the eggs with the reserved milk. Add salt and pepper and pour over the meat. Top with the fruit or bay leaves and return to the oven. Bake for a further 45 minutes, or until the top is set and lightly browned. Serve hot straight from the dish.

NANETTE

Baked Ham in Apple Juice

SERVES ABOUT 10

2–2.5 kg (4½–5 lb) joint smoked middle gammon, soaked overnight

apple juice

Demerara sugar

Orange and Lemon Sauce:

grated rind and juice of 1 lemon

juice of 3 oranges

2 tablespoons redcurrant jelly

1 tablespoon made mustard

1 tablespoon vinegar

1 tablespoon creamed horseradish

Place the gammon in a large pan and cover with apple juice. Bring to the boil, reduce the heat and simmer gently for three-quarters of the calculated cooking time, allowing 25 minutes per 450 g (1 lb). Drain, reserving the cooking juices.

Remove the outer skin and score the fat attractively in a diamond pattern with a sharp knife. Sprinkle with Demerara sugar and press into the skin. Place in a roasting tin with a little of the reserved apple juice. Bake in a preheated oven, 160°C/325°F (gas mark 3), for the remaining cooking time.

Meanwhile, to make the sauce, mix the lemon rind with the lemon and orange juices, redcurrant jelly, mustard, vinegar and horseradish. Heat gently until well blended. Serve warm with the hot sliced ham. The nice thing about this recipe is that the ham and sauce are equally good cold.

SARAH

Calf's Liver with Rosemary

SERVES 4

50 g (2 oz) butter

1 tablespoon grated onion

4 large thin slices calf's liver

2 tablespoons chopped fresh rosemary

salt

freshly ground black pepper

2 tablespoons dry sherry or light meat stock

fresh rosemary sprigs

Melt the butter in a heavy-based frying pan. Add the onion and sauté. Add the liver and sprinkle with half of the rosemary and salt and pepper. Cook gently for 3 minutes until golden on the underside. Turn over, sprinkle with the remaining rosemary and salt and pepper. Cook for a further 2 minutes or until done.

Remove from the pan and arrange on a warmed serving dish. Stir the sherry or stock into the pan juices. Cook for 1 minute to reduce slightly then pour over the cooked liver. Put a few rosemary sprigs on top of the liver and serve with lemon wedges to squeeze over.

Side Orders

When vegetables are young and fresh, you can't beat steaming them with nothing more elaborate than perhaps a sprinkling of herbs. However, when they are not at their peak, they need a bit of dressing up – here are some ways of doing it.

Nanette

NANETTE

Courgette Cream

A friend of mine grew masses of courgettes, and consequently was always thinking of new ways to serve them – this, I think, was one of the nicest.

SERVES 4–6

550 g (1¼ lb) courgettes, trimmed
sea salt
1 teaspoon cider vinegar
300 ml (½ pint) double cream
1 large egg (size 1, 2)
salt
freshly ground black pepper
50 g (2 oz) fresh breadcrumbs
15 g (½ oz) butter

Grate the courgettes into a bowl. Sprinkle with sea salt and the vinegar and leave to stand for 20 minutes. With your hands, gently squeeze out all the excess liquid and place in a buttered shallow ovenproof dish.

Beat the cream with the egg and season with salt and pepper. Pour over the courgettes and stir to mix. Bake in a preheated oven, 190°C/375°F (gas mark 5), for 25 minutes.

Remove from the oven, sprinkle with the breadcrumbs and dot with the butter. Put under a hot grill for a couple of minutes.

NANETTE

Courgettes and Apples

SERVES 4

50 g (2 oz) butter
1 onion, peeled and finely chopped
50 g (2 oz) fresh white breadcrumbs
350 g (12 oz) courgettes, trimmed and sliced
1 apple, peeled, cored and finely chopped
salt
freshly ground black pepper

Melt half of the butter in a pan. Stir in the onion and sauté until soft. Remove with a slotted spoon and reserve.

Add half of the remaining butter and heat to melt. Stir in the breadcrumbs and sauté until golden. Remove from the pan and reserve.

Add the remaining butter to the pan and melt. Stir in the courgettes and apple and cook until just tender.

Return the cooked onion to the pan with the breadcrumbs and salt and pepper. Stir and serve.

If desperately out of flowers, but you want a different table centrepiece, try filling a shallow basket with globe artichokes, shiny red peppers, lemons and lots of stems of mint and rosemary (or any other sweet-smelling herb).

Nanette

Side Orders

BAKED SWEET POTATOES WITH SOURED CREAM AND CHIVES

Side Orders

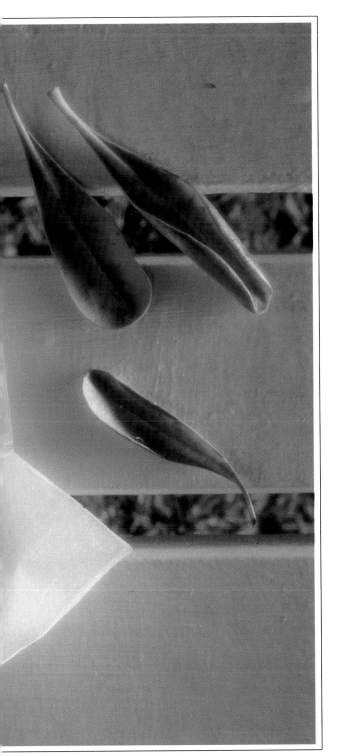

SARAH

Baked Sweet Potatoes with Soured Cream and Chives

SERVES 4–6

1 kg (2 lb) sweet potatoes or yams, scrubbed
1 tablespoon butter
4 tablespoons soured cream
2 tablespoons chopped fresh chives

Rub the sweet potato or yam skins with the butter. Bake in a preheated oven, 220°C/425°F (gas mark 7), for 30 minutes. Prick the skins with a fork and continue to bake until tender.

Remove from the oven, split and gently squeeze up the flesh. Place in a warmed serving dish. Top with the soured cream mixed with the chives. Serve hot.

SARAH: Marshmallow Sweet Potatoes: Use one medium sweet potato per person. Rub the sweet potato skins with oil and prick with a fork. Bake in a preheated oven, 220°C/425°F (gas mark 7), until tender. Remove from the oven and cut in half carefully. Scoop out the soft flesh into a bowl and mash with some butter and salt to taste. Pile back into the sweet potato skins and top each half with three white marshmallows. Return to the oven and bake until the marshmallows are melted and bubbly.

NANETTE

Red Cabbage with Marrow and Prunes

SERVES 4–6

900 g (2 lb) red cabbage, coarsely shredded or grated
50 g (2 oz) butter
225 g (8 oz) marrow, peeled and sliced (with seeds)
100 g (4 oz) pitted prunes, chopped
3 tablespoons lemon juice
250 ml (8 fl oz) apple juice
1 tablespoon soft brown sugar
salt
freshly ground black pepper

Blanch the cabbage in boiling salted water for 2–3 minutes. Drain thoroughly.

Melt the butter in a pan. Add the marrow and sauté until softened. Stir in the cabbage, prunes, lemon juice, apple juice, sugar and salt and pepper.

Spoon into a medium casserole dish, cover and cook in a preheated oven, 180°C/350°F (gas mark 4), for 45–60 minutes, stirring halfway through the cooking time. Serve hot.

NANETTE

Sautéed Radishes

SERVES 2–4

15 g (½ oz) butter
1 large bunch of radishes, trimmed and sliced
2 tablespoons soured cream
1 teaspoon coarse sea salt

Melt the butter in a pan. Add the radishes and cook until just tender, about 8 minutes, stirring occasionally.

Drain away any excess juices, stir in the soured cream and sprinkle with sea salt. Serve at once.

Souffléed Onion is a delicious and interesting vegetable side dish to serve with roasts and grills. Sauté about 2 medium chopped onions in 40 g/1½ oz butter until soft but not brown. Sprinkle with 40 g/1½ oz flour and stir to mix. Gradually add 100 ml/4 fl oz milk and 100 g/4 oz grated cheese and stir well. Add 3 beaten egg yolks, mixing well. Remove from the heat and fold in 3 stiffly-beaten egg whites with seasoning. Pour into a medium buttered ovenproof dish and bake in a preheated oven, 160°C/325°F (gas mark 3), for 30–40 minutes or until puffed up and lightly browned. Serve at once. Serves 4.

Nanette

SARAH

Braised Fennel Italian-style

SERVES 4

2 heads of fennel
50 g (2 oz) butter, melted
3 tablespoons freshly-grated Parmesan cheese
1 clove of garlic, peeled and crushed
salt
freshly ground black pepper
2 tomatoes, skinned and chopped
2 rashers back bacon, rinded and chopped
chopped fresh parsley

Trim the stems and outer leaves off the fennel, reserving the frilly leaves. Cut each fennel head into three equal slices. Cook in boiling water for 2 minutes, then drain thoroughly.

Coat the fennel slices in the melted butter and arrange in a shallow ovenproof dish. Sprinkle with the Parmesan cheese, garlic and salt and pepper. Cover with the chopped tomatoes and bacon.

Bake, uncovered, in a preheated oven, 180°C/350°F (gas mark 4), for 20–25 minutes or until the fennel is tender and the topping is crisp and browned. Sprinkle with chopped parsley and decorate with the reserved frilly fennel leaves. Serve hot with grilled meat or fish.

EMMA

Stir-fried French Beans

SERVES 4

2 tablespoons sunflower or sesame oil
450 g (1 lb) thin French or Kenyan beans, topped, tailed and halved
2 rashers smoked back bacon, rinded and chopped
4 spring onions, trimmed and sliced
1 clove of garlic, peeled and crushed
100 g (4 oz) mushrooms, wiped and quartered
50 g (2 oz) canned waterchestnuts, sliced
1 tablespoon soy sauce
1 tablespoon dry sherry
freshly ground black pepper

Heat the oil in a large heavy-based frying pan or wok. Add the beans and bacon and stir-fry for 2–3 minutes.

Stir in the spring onions, garlic and mushrooms and stir-fry for a further 5 minutes.

Add the waterchestnuts, soy sauce, sherry and pepper to taste, blending well. Stir-fry for a further 1 minute. Serve at once. This is delicious with spareribs and grilled or roasted meat and poultry.

EMMA

Greek Stuffed Tomatoes

This is a light meal in itself or a tasty vegetable accompaniment. The inspiration for the recipe came during a holiday in Greece where baked stuffed tomatoes are served in countless ways – this is my favourite.

SERVES 4

4 very large tomatoes
8 tablespoons cooked long-grain rice
salt
freshly ground black pepper
1 tablespoon sunflower oil
1 clove of garlic, peeled and crushed
275 g (10 oz) button mushrooms, wiped and finely chopped
1 teaspoon cornflour
50 g (2 oz) grated cheese
fresh parsley sprigs

Lightly grease an ovenproof dish. Cut the tops off the tomatoes and carefully scoop out the flesh using a teaspoon. Leave the tomato shells to drain, upside-down, on absorbent paper for a few minutes.

Chop the flesh of two of the tomatoes and place in a bowl with the rice and salt and pepper (use the remaining flesh for another dish). Heat the oil in a small pan, add the garlic and mushrooms and sauté but don't let the garlic brown. Stir in the cornflour, blending well. Add to the rice mixture and mix thoroughly. Spoon the mixture into the tomato shells and place in the dish. Sprinkle with the cheese and replace the tomato lids.

Bake in a preheated oven, 190°C/375°F (gas mark 5), for 15–20 minutes. Serve at once with parsley on top.

GREEK STUFFED TOMATOES

Side Orders

SARAH

Herbed Ratatouille

SERVES 4–6

2 medium aubergines, cubed
salt
5 tablespoons olive oil
2 large onions, peeled and thinly sliced
2 red peppers, cored, seeded and sliced
2 cloves of garlic, peeled and crushed
1 teaspoon ground coriander
3 large tomatoes, skinned and chopped
freshly ground black pepper
2 tablespoons chopped fresh basil

Place the aubergines in a colander or sieve and sprinkle with salt. Leave to stand for 1 hour to remove any bitter juices then rinse and drain thoroughly.

Heat the oil in a large pan. Add the onions and sauté until softened but don't allow to brown. Stir in the peppers, aubergine, garlic and coriander. Cover and simmer for about 40 minutes until everything is just tender but don't let it become mushy.

Stir in the tomatoes and season with salt and pepper. Cover and cook for a further 5 minutes. Add the basil and mix well. Serve warm or cold.

NANETTE

Steamed Carrots with Fennel and Hazelnuts

SERVES 4

450 g (1 lb) young baby carrots, trimmed
25 g (1 oz) butter
1 tablespoon chopped fresh fennel
25 g (1 oz) hazelnuts, toasted and chopped

Steam the carrots until tender, about 10–15 minutes depending upon size and maturity. Toss in the butter, fennel and hazelnuts. Spoon into a warmed serving dish.

STEAMED CARROTS WITH FENNEL AND HAZELNUTS

Side Orders

EMMA

Gingered Vegetables

Crisp and full of flavour, this is ideal to serve as part of a Chinese-style meal. It will also go well with plain grilled fish.

SERVES 4–6

2 tablespoons sunflower or sesame oil
1 onion, peeled and sliced
2 courgettes, trimmed and sliced
2 carrots, peeled and thinly sliced
1 red or yellow pepper, cored, seeded and thinly sliced
1 green pepper, cored, seeded and thinly sliced
100 g (4 oz) fresh or canned mini corn cobs
small piece of root ginger, peeled and chopped
100 g (4 oz) mangetout, trimmed
1½ teaspoons cornflour
4 tablespoons light soy sauce
2 tablespoons dry sherry
½ teaspoon Chinese 5 spice powder

Heat the oil in a large frying pan or wok. Add the onion, courgettes, carrots, peppers, corn cobs and ginger. Stir-fry for 4 minutes until almost tender but still crisp.

Add the mangetout and stir-fry for a further 1 minute. Blend the cornflour with the soy sauce, sherry and Chinese 5 spice powder. Stir into the vegetable mixture and stir-fry for 1–2 minutes until the juices are clear and thickened. Serve at once.

SARAH	NANETTE

Spinach and Bacon Salad

SERVES 4–6

450 g (1 lb) young spinach leaves, trimmed, washed and dried

6 spring onions, trimmed and finely chopped

1 tablespoon safflower or sunflower oil

1 clove of garlic, peeled and crushed

3 thin rashers bacon, rinded

1 tablespoon sugar

1 tablespoon white wine vinegar

1 tablespoon red wine vinegar

1 egg, beaten

freshly ground black pepper

Tear the spinach leaves into small pieces and place in a serving bowl with the spring onions. Mash the oil with the garlic and leave to stand while preparing the rest of the salad. Dry-fry the bacon slowly in a frying pan until very crisp. Remove and drain on absorbent paper. Allow to cool then crumble.

Beat the sugar with the vinegars, egg and pepper to taste. Stir into the warm bacon fat and cook, over a very gentle heat, for a few seconds until lightly thickened.

Add the bacon to the spinach mixture with the strained garlic oil. Pour the warm dressing over the top and toss to coat. Serve immediately.

Orange, Beetroot and Chicory Salad

SERVES 4–6

2 heads of chicory, trimmed and separated into leaves

3 medium to large cooked beetroot, peeled and thinly sliced

3 large oranges, peeled, pith removed and thinly sliced

Dressing:

4 tablespoons sunflower oil

2 tablespoons cider vinegar

1 teaspoon Dijon mustard

1 teaspoon sugar

small bunch of fresh mint, finely chopped

salt

freshly ground black pepper

Arrange the chicory, beetroot and oranges in a circular pattern on a large serving dish, slightly overlapping the layers.

To make the dressing, shake the oil with the vinegar, mustard, sugar, mint and salt and pepper to taste in a screw-topped jar.

About 10 minutes before serving, spoon the dressing over the salad.

Liven up any mixed salad combination with this fresh-tasting dressing: place the flesh from 1 large grapefruit (pink or ruby is nicest) in a blender or food processor with 100 ml (4 fl oz) salad oil, 2 teaspoons white wine vinegar and a few fresh mint leaves. Blend until well mixed.

Nanette

NANETTE

Warm Onion Salad

SERVES 4–6

6 medium onions
Dressing:
150 ml (¼ pint) walnut oil
3 tablespoons wine vinegar
½ teaspoon Dijon mustard
salt
freshly ground black pepper
1 teaspoon caraway seeds
1 tablespoon chopped fresh parsley

Place the onions, unpeeled, in a shallow ovenproof dish and bake in a preheated oven, 200°C/400°F (gas mark 6), until tender, about 40–60 minutes. Cool until warm enough to handle then remove the skins and cut into quarters. Separate the onion slices and place in a serving bowl.

To make the dressing, beat the oil with the vinegar, mustard and salt and pepper to taste. Spoon over the still warm onions and toss to coat.

Sprinkle with the caraway seeds and parsley and serve warm. This is delicious with cold meats.

Side Orders

WARM ONION SALAD

EMMA

Mushroom and Waterchestnut Salad

SERVES 4

100 g (4 oz) button mushrooms, wiped and sliced
225 g (8 oz) can waterchestnuts, drained and sliced
1 green pepper, cored, seeded and sliced
4 spring onions, trimmed and sliced
175 g (6 oz) Chinese leaves, shredded
2 tablespoons sunflower seeds
Dressing:
2 tablespoons mayonnaise
2 tablespoons natural yoghurt
2 teaspoons chopped fresh chives
salt
freshly ground black pepper

Place the mushrooms, waterchestnuts, pepper, spring onions, Chinese leaves and sunflower seeds in a salad bowl. Toss gently until well mixed. This can be prepared a little while ahead if tightly covered and stored in the refrigerator.

To make the dressing, blend the mayonnaise with the yoghurt, chives and salt and pepper to taste. Spoon over the salad just before serving and toss well.

SARAH: Mushroom and Apple Salad: Prepare as above but use 2 cored, quartered and sliced green dessert apples instead of the waterchestnuts. Vary the dressing by using soured cream instead of mayonnaise.

Home-made Mayonnaise

MAKES ABOUT 300 ML (½ PINT)

2 egg yolks
½–1 teaspoon mustard powder
½ teaspoon sugar
salt
freshly ground black pepper
300 ml (½ pint) olive oil
**2 tablespoons lemon juice or white wine
vinegar**

Place the egg yolks, mustard powder, sugar
and salt and pepper in a large bowl. Using a
balloon whisk or fork beat the mixture until
smooth. Add half of the oil, drop by drop,
beating continuously, until thick. Stir in half
of the lemon juice or wine vinegar, blending
well. Whisk in the remaining oil, drop by
drop, until the mixture is thick and glossy. Stir
in the remaining lemon juice or wine vinegar
and taste and adjust the seasoning if necessary.
Cover and chill until required.

* For a lighter mayonnaise, use sunflower,
safflower or corn oil. Home-made mayonnaise
will keep in the refrigerator for up to 1 week.

Watercress Mayonnaise

This is a quick and useful dressing for fish
and salads. It is nicer with home-made
mayonnaise, but don't worry if you make it
with a bought one – it will still taste good.

MAKES ABOUT 300 ML (½ PINT)

1 bunch of watercress, trimmed and sorted
250 ml (8 fl oz) mayonnaise
2 teaspoons double cream
salt
freshly ground black pepper

Finely chop the watercress by hand or in a
food processor then transfer to a bowl. Add
the mayonnaise, cream and salt and pepper.
Mix together well. Cover and chill until
required.

I often experiment with making different
dressings to ring the changes when
serving salads and this is a new-found
favourite. Whirl 150 ml (¼ pint) walnut
oil, 2 tablespoons raspberry vinegar, 2
tablespoons freshly-squeezed orange juice,
1 teaspoon clear honey, the grated rind of
1 orange, 2 tablespoons chopped fresh mint
leaves and salt and pepper to taste in a
blender or food processor, for about ½
minute, or until well mixed. This is
especially good with chicory leaves and
sliced oranges.

Sarah

Side Orders

EMMA

Summer Potato Salad

This is my very favourite potato salad – perfect with cold roast chicken for summertime eating.

SERVES 4–6

1 kg (2 lb) new baby potatoes, scrubbed
½ red pepper, cored, seeded and chopped
½ cucumber, chopped
4 rashers cooked streaky bacon, crumbled
2 tablespoons Greek yoghurt
1 tablespoon mayonnaise
1 tablespoon chopped fresh mint
salt
freshly ground black pepper

Cook the potatoes in their skins in boiling salted water until tender, about 12–15 minutes. Drain and allow to cool.

Place the potatoes in a serving dish with the pepper, cucumber and bacon.

Mix the yoghurt with the mayonnaise, mint and salt and pepper. Add to the potato mixture and toss gently.

Side Orders

NANETTE

The Very Best Potato Salad

Potato salad can be very boring – this one isn't!

SERVES 6

8 slices streaky bacon, rinded
1 kg (2 lb) very small new potatoes, scrubbed
6 spring onions, trimmed and chopped
3 tablespoons chopped fresh mint
1 small stick of celery, finely chopped
2 tablespoons soured cream
2 tablespoons home-made mayonnaise (see page 169)
salt
freshly ground black pepper
1 Iceberg lettuce, shredded
fresh mint sprigs to decorate

Grill the bacon until very crisp, drain on absorbent paper then crumble. Cook the potatoes in their skins in boiling salted water until tender, about 12–15 minutes. Drain and cool.

Place the potatoes in a bowl with the spring onions, bacon, mint and celery. Mix the soured cream with the mayonnaise and season with salt and pepper. Add to the potato mixture and toss lightly.

Spoon into a serving bowl lined with the chopped lettuce. Decorate with mint sprigs to serve.

SARAH: The Ultimate Potato Salad: I make my mother's potato salad but serve it in an oil and vinegar dressing, sprinkled with chopped nuts. Chopped lightly salted pecans are very good.

Afterthoughts

Everyone today is conscious of their diet. We know about additives, cholesterol, vitamins, fibre and calories – and hardly a week goes by when we don't read about some food that is harmful. However, in spite of all that, we still fall prey to temptation every now and again.

Desserts are not a necessity and they are probably not wise, but just occasionally we all throw caution to the wind and enjoy something frivolous.

You don't need a cook book to tell you how to prepare a pear or a peach, to make a fruit salad, or to hull a strawberry. These are nature's own desserts and are the most delicious of all (while also having the bonus of being good for you).

However, when temptation is strong and you feel the need for something more sinful, one of the following will fit the bill.

Nanette

Afterthoughts

Proper Puddings

EMMA

Rhubarb and Strawberry Crumble

This is a recipe from a great friend of mine, Angela, who knows that the way to my heart is through fattening puddings!

SERVES 4 GREEDY PEOPLE!

50 g (2 oz) butter
100 g (4 oz) plain wholewheat flour
50 g (2 oz) brown sugar
pinch of ground nutmeg
450 g (1 lb) rhubarb, trimmed and chopped
225 g (8 oz) strawberries, hulled
extra brown sugar (optional)

Rub half of the butter into the flour until the mixture resembles fine breadcrumbs. Stir in the sugar and nutmeg.

Cook the rhubarb in a little sweetened water until softened. Drain and place in a medium ovenproof dish with the strawberries. Top with the prepared crumble mixture. Sprinkle with a some extra brown sugar if you like and dot with the remaining butter.

Bake in a preheated oven, 190°C/375°F (gas mark 5), for 45 minutes. Serve plain or with custard, cream, ice cream or yoghurt.

SARAH

Apple, Banana and Raspberry Crunch

SERVES 4

450 g (1 lb) cooking apples, peeled, cored and cut into small chunks
3 large firm bananas, peeled and sliced
juice of 1 lemon
100 g (4 oz) raspberries, hulled
75 g (3 oz) caster sugar
Topping:
225 g (8 oz) soft brown sugar
150 g (5 oz) plain flour
75 g (3 oz) hazelnuts or walnuts, chopped
50 g (2 oz) muesli
100 g (4 oz) butter

Mix the apples with the bananas, lemon juice, raspberries and sugar. Spoon into a medium ovenproof dish.

To make the topping, mix the sugar with the flour, walnuts and muesli. Melt the butter and add to the dry ingredients, mixing well. Spoon over the fruit mixture.

Bake in a preheated oven, 180°C/350°F (gas mark 4), for 40 minutes, or until golden and bubbly. Serve hot with vanilla yoghurt.

NANETTE

Patriotic Pudding

This was served at a friend's home in America before watching an English football match. Why it's patriotic I don't know. We certainly were. Sadly England lost, but the recipe is a winner.

SERVES 6

100 g (4 oz) butter
100 g (4 oz) caster sugar
2 eggs, beaten
175 g (6 oz) plain flour
1½ teaspoons baking powder
3 very ripe bananas, peeled and mashed
2 tablespoons brown rum
grated rind of 1 orange

Cream the butter with the sugar until pale and fluffy. Add the eggs, a little at a time, with 1 tablespoon of the flour. Sift the remaining flour with the baking powder and fold into the creamed mixture. Stir in the bananas, rum and orange rind.

Spoon into a well-buttered 1.2-litre (2-pint) pudding basin. Cover with a circle of buttered greaseproof paper and a piece of greased foil which has been pleated to allow for expansion. Secure with string. Place in a steamer or on a trivet in a saucepan half-full of water and steam, over a moderate heat, for 1¾ hours.

To serve, invert the pudding onto a warmed serving dish. Serve with thick chilled cream and slices of banana, if liked, or with custard.

PATRIOTIC PUDDING

SARAH

Tricia's Apple Crisp

This recipe was given to me by a great friend. It's terribly quick, incredibly good and very, very easy. It serves eight and must be served with the best vanilla ice cream. It's really an American version of our apple crumble.

SERVES 8

6 Granny Smith apples, peeled, cored and very thinly sliced
juice of 3 lemons
175 g (6 oz) plain flour
2½ teaspoons ground cinnamon
pinch of salt
175 g (6 oz) butter
350 g (12 oz) soft brown sugar
50 g (2 oz) pecans, chopped
50 g (2 oz) walnuts, chopped

Layer the apples in a 20-cm (8-inch) greased round cake tin or 25 × 15-cm (8 × 6-inch) rectangular baking dish, sprinkling lemon juice between each layer.

Sift the flour with the cinnamon and salt. Rub in the butter until the mixture resembles fine breadcrumbs. Stir in the sugar and nuts.

Spoon evenly over the apple mixture, pressing down firmly.

Bake in a preheated oven, 180°C/350°F (gas mark 4), for 50–60 minutes, or until the apples are cooked and the topping is crisp and golden brown.

Serve hot with ice cream.

In America we can easily buy blueberries and, although not so readily available, you can get them in England. I like to serve them with a crunchy crumble and call the recipe Blueberry Hotch Potch: Simply rub 50 g (2 oz) butter into 100 g (4 oz) plain flour then stir in 50 g (2 oz) sugar. Spread on a baking tray and bake in a preheated oven, 200°C/ 400°F (gas mark 6), for about 12 minutes, stirring with a fork from time to time. Meanwhile, gently heat about 450 g (1 lb) blueberries until just warm. Mix with the cooked crumble and serve immediately.

Sarah

Afterthoughts

SARAH

Upside-down Ginger Pudding

This is a real 'nursery' pudding, elevated to grown-up status by serving it with a special creamy adult-only sauce.

SERVES 6

Topping:
50 g (2 oz) butter
100 g (4 oz) soft dark brown sugar
3 medium pears, peeled and cored

Base:
100 g (4 oz) plain flour
½ teaspoon bicarbonate of soda
1 teaspoon ground ginger
pinch of ground nutmeg
pinch of ground cloves
pinch of salt
2 teaspoons ground cinnamon
1 egg, beaten
100 g (4 oz) brown sugar
75 g (3 oz) black treacle
100 ml (4 fl oz) milk
2 teaspoons lemon juice
50 g (2 oz) butter or margarine, melted

Sauce:
150 ml (¼ pint) double cream, whipped
150 ml (¼ pint) natural yoghurt
1 tablespoon caster sugar

To make the topping, melt the butter in a pan. Add the sugar and cook for 2 minutes. Pour into a 20-cm (8-inch) round cake tin. Cut each pear lengthways into eight pieces. Place over the topping in an attractive pattern.

To make the base, sift the flour with the bicarbonate of soda, ginger, nutmeg, cloves, salt and cinnamon. Beat the egg with the sugar, treacle, milk and lemon juice. Stir into the flour mixture with the butter or margarine and mix well. Spoon evenly over the pears to cover.

Bake in a preheated oven, 190°C/375°F (gas mark 5), for 50–70 minutes, or until well-risen, golden brown and cooked.

Meanwhile to make the sauce, mix the cream with the yoghurt and caster sugar. To serve, invert the pudding onto a warmed serving plate. Serve while still warm with the creamy sauce.

Afterthoughts

NANETTE

Hip-hugging Pudding

For those men who get misty-eyed about syrup pudding, or spotted dick, and all those other desserts reminiscent of school lunches, here is a pudding that will gladden their hearts (if put inches on their hips!)

SERVES 8–10

25 g (1 oz) plain flour
75 g (3 oz) sultanas
50 g (2 oz) ground almonds
½ teaspoon ground cloves
½ teaspoon ground cinnamon
50 g (2 oz) walnuts, chopped
1 small apple, peeled and grated
100 g (4 oz) sugar
6 eggs, separated

Mix the flour with the sultanas, ground almonds, cloves, cinnamon, walnuts, apple and sugar. Add the egg yolks, one at a time, mixing well. Whisk the egg whites until they stand in stiff peaks. Fold into the mixture. Spoon into a buttered 1.8-litre (3-pint) ring mould or baking tin.

Bake in a preheated oven, 180°C/350°F (gas mark 4), for 40–50 minutes, until well-risen, golden and cooked. Serve hot with proper custard.

NANETTE

Proper Custard

SERVES 4–6

2 large egg yolks (size 1, 2)
300 ml (½ pint) milk
1 tablespoon sugar
1 vanilla pod

Beat the egg yolks in a bowl. Heat the milk with the sugar and vanilla pod until almost boiling. Remove the vanilla pod and pour the milk over the egg yolks, mixing well. Return to the pan and cook, over a low heat, until the custard thickens slightly (or will thinly coat the back of a spoon), stirring frequently. Serve warm or cold.

Afterthoughts

EMMA

School Pudding

I am one of the very few people who actually loved school food. So much so that I was really put out during one period of my school life when my mother went on a great health kick – I was given packed lunches that consisted of wholewheat bread and things like alfalfa, sprouted mung beans and yeast extract. I used to look so longingly at the school lunch toad-in-the-hole, spotted dick and roly-poly pudding with lumpy custard that in the end Mummy succumbed. Although I now (in the perverse way we children have) eat healthy food from choice, once a year I indulge my nostalgia with this School Pudding and some (not very) lumpy custard.

SERVES 6

100 g (4 oz) fresh breadcrumbs
100 g (4 oz) shredded suet
25 g (1 oz) plain flour
75 g (3 oz) sugar
75 g (3 oz) apricot jam
75 g (3 oz) sultanas
juice of 1 lemon
grated rind of 2 lemons
3 eggs, beaten

Mix the breadcrumbs with the suet, flour, sugar, jam, sultanas, lemon juice and rind. Add the eggs, beating well to make a smooth mixture.

Spoon into a well-buttered 1.2-litre (2-pint) pudding basin. Cover with a circle of buttered greaseproof paper and a piece of greased foil pleated to allow for expansion. Secure with string. Place in a steamer or on a trivet in a saucepan half-full of water and steam, over a moderate heat, for 1 hour.

To serve, invert the pudding onto a warmed serving dish. Serve with custard, yoghurt, ice cream or cream.

Afterthoughts

NANETTE

Sweet Flan Pastry

This is the pastry recipe I use for sweet flans and tarts. Everyone has a favourite recipe, if you have one, use it.

MAKES 1 QUANTITY PASTRY, ENOUGH TO LINE A 23-CM (9-INCH) FLAN OR TART

225 g (8 oz) plain flour
pinch of salt
150 g (5 oz) butter
2 teaspoons icing sugar
1 egg yolk
few drops of iced water

Put the flour, salt, butter, icing sugar and egg yolk in a food processor and process until the mixture is crumbly, about ½ minute. Add a few drops of water, with the motor running, and process until the mixture forms a dough ball. Wrap in clingfilm and chill for 30 minutes before using.

Alternatively, sift the flour with the salt into a bowl. Rub in the butter until the mixture resembles fine breadcrumbs. Stir in the sugar, egg yolk and a few drops of water and bind to a smooth dough. Knead lightly and chill as before.

* I always roll out this pastry between two sheets of greaseproof paper – it stops it from sticking but you can roll it out in the usual way if you wish.

SARAH

Pecan Pie

Pecan Pie is as American as Apple Pie is English – only better.

SERVES 8

1 quantity Sweet Flan Pastry (see this page)
5 eggs
50 g (2 oz) muscovado sugar
1 teaspoon vanilla essence
25 g (1 oz) butter, melted
475 ml (16 fl oz) maple syrup
25 g (1 oz) plain flour
grated rind of 1 lemon
100 g (4 oz) pecan halves

Roll out the pastry and use to line a 23-cm (9-inch) pie plate or flan dish.

Beat the eggs with the sugar and vanilla essence until thick and glossy. Stir in the butter, maple syrup and flour, mixing well. Pour into the pastry case and sprinkle with the lemon rind. Top with the pecan halves – don't worry if they appear to float.

Bake in a preheated oven, 180°C/350°F (gas mark 4), for about 50 minutes, or until the filling has set and the pastry is cooked. Allow to cool then chill thoroughly.

Serve this very sweet pie with chilled whipped cream or vanilla ice cream.

Afterthoughts

NANETTE

Chocolate Pie

SERVES 4–6

Base:

50 g (2 oz) butter

50 g (2 oz) sugar

350 g (12 oz) rolled oats

40 g (1½ oz) plain flour

Filling:

450 g (1 lb) cream cheese

175 g (6 oz) caster sugar

2 eggs, beaten

100 g (4 oz) plain chocolate, melted

2 teaspoons coffee powder

1 tablespoon hot water

150 ml (¼ pint) soured cream

1 teaspoon vanilla essence

grated chocolate

To make the base, cream the butter with the sugar until light and fluffy. Stir in the oats and flour. Press the mixture onto the base of a lightly-greased 23-cm (9-inch) loose-bottomed cake tin. Bake in a preheated oven, 200°C/400°F (gas mark 6), for 15 minutes.

To make the filling, cream the cheese with the sugar until light and fluffy. Gradually add the eggs, mixing well. Fold in the chocolate, coffee dissolved in the water, soured cream and vanilla essence. Pour onto the cooked base.

Reduce the oven temperature to 160°C/325°F (gas mark 3), and bake the pie for a further 40 minutes, or until firm to the touch. Remove from the oven and allow to cool.

When cool sprinkle with finely grated plain chocolate.

I brought both my daughters up on 'healthy' food – wholemeal bread, vegetables and fruit being the mainstay of their diet, and hardly any sweets or chocolate. *I say* this is why they have beautiful skins and great teeth.

They say it's why they now go on chocolate binges, because they were deprived. Ah, well! you just can't win.

Nanette

SARAH

Key Lime Pie

This is America's answer to Lemon Meringue Pie; and if you think anything this easy can't taste as good as it does – you're wrong!

SERVES 6

Base:
100 g (4 oz) wheatmeal digestive biscuits, crushed
2 teaspoons sugar
50 g (2 oz) butter, melted
Filling:
6 egg yolks
juice of 4–5 limes or 250 ml (8 fl oz) lime juice
2 × 400 g (14 oz) cans sweetened condensed milk
2 tablespoons grated lime rind
whipped cream
lime slices

To make the base, mix the biscuit crumbs with the sugar. Stir in the butter and press firmly onto the base and sides of a 23-cm (9-inch) pie plate or flan dish (lined with foil if liked to make removal from the tin easy).

To make the filling, beat the egg yolks with the lime juice, condensed milk and lime rind.

Pour into the biscuit crust and freeze overnight.

To serve, remove from the freezer, top with the whipped cream and decorate with slices and twists of lime.

Allow to stand for a bit before cutting to serve.

Blackberry Tart makes a super late summer dessert. Chop 150 g (5 oz) walnuts in a food processor. Add 175 g (6 oz) plain flour and 100 g (4 oz) butter and process briefly. Add 60 g (2½ oz) sugar and 1 egg and process until the mixture holds together. Chill for about 20 minutes then press into a 23-cm (9-inch) flan tin or dish. Bake in a preheated oven, 180°C/350°F (gas mark 4), for 20 minutes and cool. When cool, pile about 450 g (1 lb) hulled blackberries into the tart crust. Melt a 175 g (6 oz) jar of blackcurrant jelly over a low heat. Sprinkle 1 dessertspoon powdered gelatine over 3 tablespoons orange juice and leave to soften. Stir into the blackcurrant jelly then leave until nearly cool and syrupy. Brush over the blackberries to glaze. Chill and serve with Greek-style yoghurt. Serves 6.

Emma

KEY LIME PIE

Afterthoughts

SARAH

Camilla's Tart

SERVES 4–6

Pastry:
175 g (6 oz) plain flour
pinch of salt
75 g (3 oz) butter
1 egg, beaten
Filling:
225 g (8 oz) cream cheese
175 g (6 oz) sugar
150 ml (¼ pint) double cream
3 eggs, beaten
50 g (2 oz) sultanas

To make the pastry, sift the flour and the salt into a bowl. Rub in the butter until the mixture resembles fine breadcrumbs. Stir in the egg and a little water if necessary to mix to a firm but pliable dough. Knead lightly until smooth. Roll out on a lightly-floured surface to a round large enough to line a 23-cm (9-inch) greased, loose-bottomed, fluted flan tin. Bake 'blind' in a preheated oven, 190°C/375°F (gas mark 5), for 10–15 minutes, to par-bake.

Meanwhile, beat the cheese with the sugar until creamy. Add the cream, eggs and sultanas, mixing well.

Pour into the part-baked flan case, return to the oven and bake for a further 25–30 minutes, until cooked and firm.

Eat plain or serve just warm topped with fresh raspberries or blueberries.

Afterthoughts

NANETTE

Temperamental Tart

This was my mother's recipe – and her name for what seems to be a very untemperamental dessert. It does occasionally resist being turned out, but other than that it's faultless.

SERVES 6

Base:
175 g (6 oz) wheatmeal digestive biscuits, crushed
75 g (3 oz) oatmeal
50 g (2 oz) Demerara sugar
50 g (2 oz) butter, melted
Filling:
175 g (6 oz) curd cheese
100 g (4 oz) caster sugar
2 eggs, separated
50 g (2 oz) sultanas
grated rind of 1 large lemon
100 g (4 oz) round-grain rice cooked in 300 ml (½ pint) milk until soft

To make the base, mix the biscuit crumbs with the oatmeal, sugar and melted butter. Press into a greased rectangular dish measuring about 23 × 15 cm (9 × 6 inches). Chill to firm.

To make the filling, beat the cheese with the sugar until pale and creamy. Beat in the egg yolks with the sultanas and lemon rind. Fold in the cooked rice.

Whisk the egg whites until they stand in stiff peaks. Fold into the rice mixture. Pour over the prepared base and bake in a preheated oven, 190°C/375°F (gas mark 5), for 35–45 minutes. Allow to cool slightly, loosen the edges with a knife then transfer to a serving dish.

Serve while still warm.

Afterthoughts

EMMA

Almond and Pear Flan

SERVES 6–8

Base:

225 g (8 oz) wheatmeal digestive biscuits, crushed

75 g (3 oz) butter, melted

Filling:

100 g (4 oz) butter

100 g (4 oz) caster sugar

3 eggs

100 g (4 oz) self-raising flour

100 g (4 oz) ground almonds

1½ tablespoons milk

½ teaspoon vanilla essence

2 large Comice pears, peeled, cored and quartered

vanilla sugar to sprinkle

25 g (1 oz) flaked almonds, toasted (optional)

To make the base, mix the digestive biscuit crumbs with the butter. Press into a 30-cm (12-inch) ovenproof flan tin or dish and chill.

To make the filling, beat the butter with the sugar until pale and creamy. Beat in the eggs, one at a time, mixing well. Fold in the flour with the almonds, milk and vanilla essence.

Plunge the pears into a bowl of boiling water, leave for ½ minute then remove.

Spoon the creamed mixture over the prepared flan base – don't worry if there does not seem to be a great deal of mixture, it does rise during cooking. Arrange the pears on top in an attractive circular pattern, pressing into the mixture. Sprinkle with a little vanilla sugar.

Bake in a preheated oven, 200°C/400°F (gas mark 6), for 20–25 minutes.

Serve warm, sprinkled with the toasted almonds if liked.

* If you can't get fresh pears then use canned.

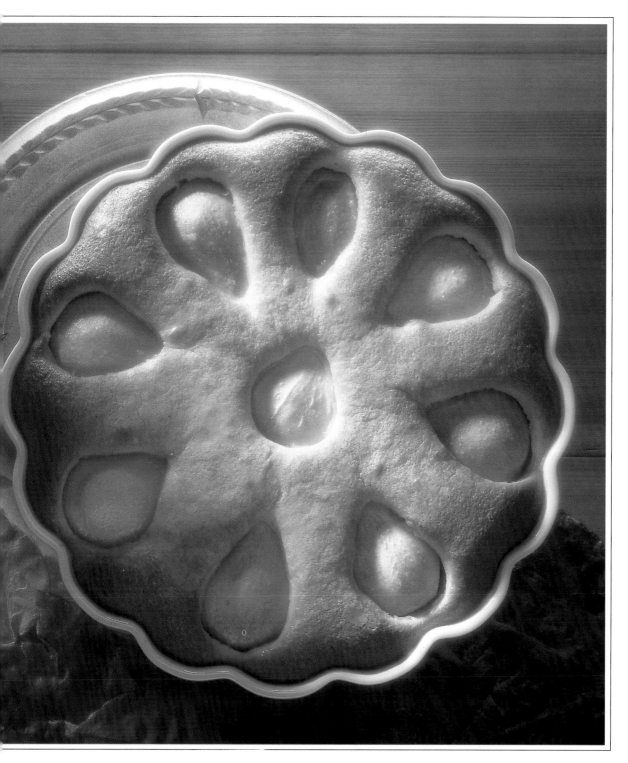

ALMOND AND PEAR FLAN

Afterthoughts

SARAH

Butterscotch Sauce for Billy Bunters

This is so truly wonderfully sickly you can only completely enjoy it if you're about to start a diet or are seriously underweight. It must be eaten with the very best vanilla ice cream; or, for non-purists, coffee-flavoured I like to eat mine alone so that no one can witness my expanding waist-line. Sprinkle with toasted almonds or sliced peaches and you'll be as close to heaven as anyone has a right to be!

SERVES 4–6

100 g (4 oz) butter
250 ml (8 fl oz) single cream
175 g (6 oz) dark brown sugar
1 tablespoon coffee powder

Melt the butter over a very low heat in the top of a double boiler. Add the cream, sugar and coffee dissolved in a little water, mixing well. Cook slowly for about 30 minutes, stirring occasionally. Remove from the heat, pour into a small bowl and leave to cool and thicken slightly.

Serve lightly chilled with ice cream. Keep what you don't eat in a jar in the refrigerator labelled 'PRIVATE'.

EMMA

After Christmas Pudding

After Christmas with my family I can guarantee that my mother will pack me off with the leftovers – including the Christmas pudding, well soaked in brandy but lacking the same appeal that it had on Christmas Day. This is what I do with it to give it a new lease of life.

Christmas pudding, finely chopped
vanilla ice cream
1 tablespoon brandy (optional)
chopped nuts

Mix the Christmas pudding with vanilla ice cream (the amount will depend upon how much pudding you have left). Stir in the brandy if liked. Spoon into a freezer-proof bowl or shallow dish, cover and freeze until firm.

Remove from the freezer about 15 minutes before required to soften slightly. Serve sliced or scooped into dishes, sprinkled with chopped nuts.

* P.S. Don't let on it's leftover Christmas pudding!

Afterthoughts

NANETTE

Black Cherry Tart

On a trip to Italy in June, we drove north from Rome to the region of Umbria, past fields of wheat and oats, castles perched on hilltops and vast stretches of sunflowers turning their yellow heads to face the sun. We arrived at Fernando's house in the afternoon and had this Cherry Tart, made locally in the village, for tea. Whenever I make it the memories flood back of that afternoon sitting on a sun-drenched terrace – knowing it was raining in England.

SERVES 6–8

Pastry:
200 g (7 oz) plain flour
90 g (3½ oz) butter
25 g (1 oz) caster sugar
3 tablespoons cold water
Filling:
700 g (1½ lb) black cherries, stoned
75 g (3 oz) plain flour
100 g (4 oz) sugar
4 eggs
300 ml (½ pint) single cream

To make the pastry, sift the flour into a bowl. Rub in the butter until the mixture resembles fine breadcrumbs. Stir in the sugar. Add sufficient water to bind to a dough. Knead lightly, wrap in clingfilm and chill for 30 minutes or until required.

Roll out the pastry and use to line a rectangular, loose-bottomed, shallow baking tin, measuring about 25 × 15 cm (10 × 6 inches). Prick and bake 'blind' in a preheated oven, 190°C/375°F (gas mark 5), for 10 minutes.

Remove the part-cooked tart base from the oven and fill with the cherries. Beat the flour with the sugar and eggs. Gradually add the cream, beating well. Pour the mixture over the cherries. Reduce the oven temperature to 180°C/350°F (gas mark 4).

Bake the tart for 30–35 minutes until the pastry is crisp and golden and the filling is cooked. Serve just warm.

Afterthoughts

Just Desserts

EMMA

Yoghurt Brulée

This is my own version of my very favourite pudding – crème brulée.

SERVES 6

150 ml (¼ pint) double cream
450 g (1 lb) Greek-style yoghurt
2 egg yolks, beaten
1 tablespoon clear honey
¼ teaspoon vanilla essence
75 g (3 oz) dark brown sugar

Mix the cream with the yoghurt, egg yolks, honey and vanilla essence in the top of a double boiler. Cook gently, stirring constantly, until the mixture will coat the back of a spoon, about 5 minutes.

Pour into six small ramekin dishes and sprinkle evenly with the sugar. Caramelise under a preheated hot grill until golden and bubbly. Allow to cool then chill thoroughly to serve, about 4–6 hours.

SARAH: For a more exotic dessert try placing 2 tablespoons puréed apricots in the base of each ramekin before adding the creamy yoghurt mixture.

EMMA

Baked Bananas with Honey and Almonds

This is a really quick, last-minute dessert, which is a great standby.

SERVES 4

4 bananas, peeled
4 tablespoons clear or creamed honey
50 g (2 oz) flaked almonds
4 teaspoons brown sugar
2 tablespoons brown rum

Slice each banana in half lengthways. Place in a shallow ovenproof dish. Drizzle over the honey and sprinkle with the almonds and sugar. Spoon over the rum, cover and bake in a preheated oven, 200°C/400°F (gas mark 6), for about 10–12 minutes until just tender and bubbly.

Serve warm with whipped cream.

EMMA

Alternative Fruit Salad

I use the very best of fruit in season for my alternative fruit salad, for example, strawberries, raspberries, bananas, apples, kiwi fruit, tangerines, grapefruit, mango and melon to name a few. Sometimes I top it with Greek-style yoghurt flavoured with honey and sprinkled with toasted almonds, but this is my very favourite topping idea.

SERVES 4–6

about 1 kg (2 lb) prepared fresh fruit
juice of 2 lemons or limes
Praline:
100 g (4 oz) brown sugar
25 g (1 oz) butter
50 g (2 oz) flaked almonds
25 g (1 oz) hazelnuts, chopped
whipped double cream to serve

Place the fruit in a serving bowl with the lemon or lime juice. Cover and chill for at least 2 hours.

Meanwhile, make the praline: place the sugar in a non-stick pan and heat gently to melt, stirring constantly. The mixture will appear lumpy to begin with but will cook smoothly. Add the butter, stirring well. Stir in the nuts and mix to coat. Pour at once onto a baking tray covered with greased foil or greaseproof paper and leave to cool.

To serve, top the fruit salad with mounds of whipped cream. Break the praline into small pieces using a rolling pin and scatter over the cream.

Serve at once.

Everyone knows I have basket-mania. I use baskets for everything – fruit, flowers, make-up, magazines, etc. I have a collection of very small baskets, found on a trip to France, that I use when strawberries are at their very best. I like to serve each guest with their own basket of strawberries, sitting in the middle of a large plate, with a small mound of thick cream on the side. Guests then help themselves to lemon or orange quarters, sugar or ground pepper.

Nanette

Afterthoughts

EMMA

Plums in Grand Marnier

SERVES 4

75 g (3 oz) caster sugar
300 ml (½ pint) water
450 g (1 lb) red plums, left whole
grated rind of 1 orange
3 tablespoons Grand Marnier

Place the sugar and water in a heavy-based pan and heat gently until the sugar dissolves. Add the plums and orange rind and simmer gently until the plums are cooked, about 10–15 minutes.

Stir in the Grand Marnier and transfer to a serving bowl. Serve warm or cold with whipped cream.

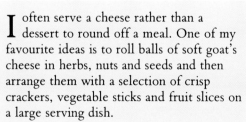

I often serve a cheese rather than a dessert to round off a meal. One of my favourite ideas is to roll balls of soft goat's cheese in herbs, nuts and seeds and then arrange them with a selection of crisp crackers, vegetable sticks and fruit slices on a large serving dish.

Sarah

Afterthoughts

PLUMS IN GRAND MARNIER

Afterthoughts

NANETTE

Orange Curaçao Meringue

SERVES 4–6

Meringue:
4 egg whites
225 g (8 oz) caster sugar
Filling:
4 egg yolks
100 g (4 oz) caster sugar
300 ml (½ pint) double cream
3 tablespoons orange curaçao liqueur
1 tablespoon chopped pistachio nuts

Line a baking tray with greased greaseproof paper or foil.

To make the meringue base, whisk the egg whites until they stand in peaks. Whisk in half of the sugar, 1 tablespoon at a time, until thick and glossy. Fold in the remaining sugar. Pipe or spoon the meringue onto the prepared tray in a round shape, making the edges of the meringue thicker than the centre (you can, of course, spoon the meringue into whatever shape you like, experiment with different shaped bases). Bake in a preheated oven, 120°C/250°F (gas mark ½), for about 2½ hours, until firm and crisp. Remove carefully from the baking tray and allow to cool on a wire rack.

To make the filling, beat the egg yolks with the sugar until pale and creamy. Place in a bowl over a pan of simmering water and cook, stirring constantly, until the mixture coats the back of a spoon, about 20–30 minutes. Remove from the heat and allow to cool.

Whip the cream until it stands in soft peaks. Fold into the cooled custard with the orange curaçao. Chill thoroughly.

To serve, fill the centre of the meringue with the chilled orange curaçao cream. Sprinkle with pistachio nuts to serve.

Afterthoughts

NANETTE

Rhubarb Cheesecake

SERVES 4–6

Base:

225 g (8 oz) ginger biscuits, crushed

25 g (1 oz) Demerara sugar

75 g (3 oz) butter, melted

Filling:

450 g (1 lb) rhubarb, trimmed and cut into even-sized pieces

175 g (6 oz) caster sugar

100 ml (4 fl oz) water

piece of pared orange rind

450 g (1 lb) cream cheese

2 eggs, beaten

150 ml (¼ pint) double cream

To make the base, mix the biscuit crumbs with the sugar. Add the butter and stir to coat. Use to line the base of a 20-cm (8-inch) greased, loose-bottomed cake tin. Chill thoroughly.

To make the filling, place the rhubarb, half of the sugar and water in a heavy-based pan. Add the orange rind and cook gently until the rhubarb is tender. Allow to cool then remove and discard the orange rind.

Beat the cream cheese with the eggs, remaining sugar and cream until thick. Add three-quarters of the cooked rhubarb and swirl to mix. Pour over the prepared biscuit base and bake in a preheated oven, 160°C/325°F (gas mark 3), for 30–40 minutes, until firm and set. Remove from the oven and allow to cool completely in the tin.

To serve, carefully unmould the cooked cheesecake from the tin and place on a serving plate. Top with the remaining rhubarb and chill thoroughly.

Serve cut into thick wedges.

Afterthoughts

SARAH

Oreo Cookie Cheesecake

If you're not married and want to be, making this cheesecake is a sure way of getting a marriage proposal fast, provided your boyfriend is thin.

SERVES 12–14

Base:

350 g (12 oz) oreo cookies (oreo cookies, although expensive, are to be found in England but if you can't get them use chocolate bourbon biscuits instead), crushed

100 g (4 oz) butter, melted

Filling:

800 g (1¾ lb) cream cheese

4 eggs, beaten

175 g (6 oz) sugar

200 ml (7 fl oz) single cream

350 g (12 oz) oreo cookies or chocolate bourbon biscuits, coarsely broken into small pieces

400 g (14 oz) soured cream

2 tablespoons sugar

Topping:

4 tablespoons soured cream

grated chocolate

To make the base, mix the crushed cookies or biscuits with the butter. Press firmly into a 30- to 35-cm (12- to 14-inch) diameter spring-form cake tin.

To make the filling, beat the cream cheese with the eggs and sugar until smooth. Stir in the cream and pour half of this filling over the prepared base. Top with the broken biscuits and press into the cheesecake mixture. Cover with the remaining cheesecake mixture. Bake in a preheated oven, 190°C/375°F (gas mark 5), for 25 minutes, or until the cheesecake is fairly well set around the edges of the tin.

Remove from the oven and increase the oven temperature to 240°C/475°F (gas mark 9). Mix the soured cream with the sugar and spread over the top of the cheesecake. Return to the oven and bake for exactly 5 minutes. Remove from the oven, allow to cool then chill thoroughly to serve.

Spread the soured cream over the cheesecake and sprinkle with grated chocolate to decorate.

Cut into wedges to serve.

OREO COOKIE CHEESECAKE

Afterthoughts

EMMA

Extra Rich Chocolate Mousse

SERVES 4

225 g (8 oz) plain chocolate
2 tablespoons liqueur (for example, brandy, rum or Tia Maria)
4 eggs, separated
whipped cream
crumbled chocolate flake bar to decorate

Break the chocolate into pieces and melt in the top of a double boiler or in a bowl over a pan of simmering water. Add the chosen liqueur and stir quickly to mix. Beat in the egg yolks, one at a time, then remove from the heat.

Whisk the egg whites until they stand in stiff peaks. Fold into the chocolate mixture. Pour into one dish or four small ramekin dishes and chill to set.

Serve topped with a little whipped cream and sprinkled with crumbled chocolate flake bar to decorate.

SARAH

Chocolate Mint Mousse

SERVES 8

3 eggs, separated
175 g (6 oz) caster sugar
3 tablespoons crème de menthe
2 teaspoons coffee powder
400 g (14 oz) plain chocolate
75 g (3 oz) butter
450 ml (¾ pint) double cream

Beat the egg yolks with the sugar until thick and creamy. Add the crème de menthe and coffee dissolved in a little hot water, mixing well.

Break the chocolate into a bowl, add the butter and melt over a pan of hot water. Add the egg yolk mixture, mixing well. Whip the cream until it stands in soft peaks and fold into the chocolate mixture.

Whisk the egg whites until they stand in stiff peaks and fold into the chocolate mixture. Pour into a 900-ml (1½-pint) serving dish or eight small wine glasses and chill to set.

Serve chilled.

Afterthoughts

NANETTE

Fresh-tasting Raspberry Mousse for Dieters

SERVES 4

100 g (4 oz) raspberries, hulled
15 g (½ oz) sugar
7 g (¼ oz) powdered gelatine
1 tablespoon boiling water
450 ml (¾ pint) thick natural yoghurt
few fresh raspberries or sliced strawberries to decorate

Purée the raspberries in a blender or food processor. Sieve to remove the pips then mix with the sugar. Dissolve the gelatine in the water and stir into the raspberry mixture.

Fold in the yoghurt and pour into a serving dish. Cover and chill for not less than 3 hours. Serve decorated with a few fresh raspberries or sliced strawberries.

NANETTE

Ritz Dessert

When I first had this at my friend, Barbara's, house I thought it was delicious but had no idea what it was.

SERVES 4–6

3 egg whites
225 g (8 oz) caster sugar
½ teaspoon baking powder
14 Ritz crackers, crushed
75 g (3 oz) walnuts, chopped
300 ml (½ pint) double cream

Whisk the egg whites until frothy. Add the sugar and baking powder, a tablespoon at a time, whisking constantly, until very stiff.

Fold in the crackers and nuts. Spoon into a greased 23-cm/9-inch pie tin or ovenproof flan dish and level the surface. Bake in a preheated oven, 160°C/325°F (gas mark 3), for 35 minutes. Remove from the oven and allow to cool then chill thoroughly, about 24 hours.

Whip the cream until it stands in soft peaks. Pile or pipe on top of the dessert to serve.

Fooled Mango is the perfect light dessert to serve after a hearty main course. Purée the flesh of 2 very ripe mangoes with the juice of 1 lime and 1 heaped tablespoon of clear honey. Whip the cream until thick and fold into the mango purée. Serve chilled in tall wine glasses. Serves 4.

Emma

Afterthoughts

SARAH

Redcurrants with Melon

SERVES 4

450 g (1 lb) redcurrants, topped and tailed
3 tablespoons sugar
1 Charentais melon

Place the redcurrants and sugar in a small pan and cook, over a very low heat, until the sugar has dissolved and the juices run from the fruit. Whirl in a blender or food processor, strain through a sieve and chill.

Peel the melon, remove the seeds and cut lengthways into very thin slices. Arrange on a large plate in a fan shape.

Carefully spoon the chilled redcurrant sauce over the melon to serve.

NANETTE

Green Gunpowder Tea Ice Cream

SERVES 4–6

150 ml (¼ pint) freshly-made strong green gunpowder tea
juice of ½ lemon
4 egg yolks
100 g (4 oz) caster sugar
600 ml (1 pint) double cream

Mix the cold tea with the lemon juice. Beat the egg yolks with the sugar until thick and creamy. Heat the cream until very hot but do not allow to boil. Beat into the egg mixture, blending well. Add the tea and stir, over a very gentle heat, until the mixture begins to thicken and will coat the back of a spoon. Allow to cool then pour into a freezer tray. Freeze until mushy, about 1–2 hours.

Remove from the freezer and whisk to break down any large ice crystals. Return to the freezer tray and freeze until firm.

Remove the ice cream from the freezer about 20 minutes before required to soften slightly. Serve scooped into chilled wine glasses.

GREEN GUNPOWDER TEA ICE CREAM

Afterthoughts

NANETTE

Melon Sorbet

SERVES 4–6

700 g (1½ lb) melon flesh
275 g (10 oz) caster sugar
300 ml (½ pint) boiling water

Purée the melon in a blender or food processor until smooth. Mix the sugar with the boiling water and stir to dissolve. Mix with the melon purée, measure and make up to 1.2 litres (2 pints) with cold water if necessary. Pour into a freezer tray and freeze for 30 minutes or until mushy.

Remove from the freezer and whisk well to break down any ice crystals. Return to the freezer tray and freeze again for a further 30 minutes. Repeat then freeze until firm.

Remove the sorbet from the freezer about 10 minutes before required to soften slightly. Serve scooped into chilled glasses.

* This is nice served in small melon shells.

EMMA

Araminta's Lemon Freeze

SERVES 6

50 g (2 oz) cornflakes, crushed
75 g (3 oz) caster sugar
50 g (2 oz) butter, melted
2 eggs, separated
170 g (6 oz) can condensed milk
150 ml (¼ pint) double cream
finely-grated rind and juice of 2 lemons

Mix the cornflakes with 50 g (2 oz) of the sugar and butter. Spoon into a medium shallow freezer tray lined with foil, reserving 2 tablespoons for the topping. Press firmly onto the base of the tray with the back of a spoon. Chill until required.

Meanwhile, to make the ice cream filling, mix the egg yolks with the condensed milk and cream until smooth and creamy. Stir in the lemon rind and juice until the mixture thickens slightly. Whisk the egg whites until they stand in stiff peaks. Whisk in the remaining sugar until the mixture is thick and glossy. Fold into the lemon mixture, pour over the prepared base and level the surface. Sprinkle with the cornflake mixture. Cover and freeze until firm, about 2–4 hours.

Remove from the freezer about 10 minutes before required to soften slightly.

Afterthoughts

EMMA

Panic Stations Dessert

An actor I know (who incidentally can't cook) makes this for dinner parties. It's rich and tastes as if a lot of effort has gone into it. In fact, anyone capable of opening a tin can make it!

SERVES 4–6

425 g (15 oz) can sweetened chestnut purée
300 ml (½ pint) double cream

Beat the chestnut purée until smooth and creamy. Whip the cream until it stands in soft peaks. Fold into the chestnut purée. Spoon into *very* small dessert glasses and chill thoroughly to serve.

ELABORATE ICE CREAM

Buy a tub of good-quality chocolate or coffee ice cream and let it soften a little. Mix together some finely-chopped toasted hazelnuts and finely-grated plain chocolate and spread out on a large sheet of greaseproof paper. Take a scoop of ice cream and form into a ball. Roll in the chocolate and hazelnut mixture, making sure that you coat the ice cream well. Place on a baking sheet lined with greaseproof paper and freeze until required. Remove from the freezer about 6–8 minutes before serving. Serve 1 per person, on a large dinner plate, resting on this sauce: Beat a small tub of whipping cream with 2 tablespoons Cointreau, the juice of half an orange and 2 teaspoons icing sugar, until just beginning to thicken. Swirl onto plates and top with the prepared ice cream.

If liked, the ice cream can be made into smaller balls, about the size of a walnut. The balls can then be served in half a poached pear.

Alternatively, push a rich chocolate truffle into the centre of the ice cream and re-shape before rolling in the chocolate and hazelnut mixture.

Nanette

If you ever need to conjure up a dessert that looks impressive, yet takes little time to prepare, make a Zabaglione. Place 4 egg yolks and 2 tablespoons caster sugar in the top of a double boiler (or a bowl set over a pan of simmering water). Beat well then add ½ glass of Marsala wine (or other sweet white wine) and keep beating until pale and very thick. Serve immediately with ratafia biscuits. Serves 4.

Nanette

Acknowledgements

All three of us would like to give an enormous thank you to Carol Bowen for all her hard work and enthusiasm – and also for being the only person ever to understand my handwriting.

Nanette

The publishers would like to thank the following shops for lending the equipment and props shown in many of the photographs:

Conran Shop,
77–79 Fulham Road,
London SW3.

N.J.A. Gifford Mead,
533 Kings Road,
London SW3.

Index

SUMMER TARTS

First make pastry - and line some tart tins (4 oz size with removable bottoms are best). Bake 'blind' - usual way - until light brown and crisp. Make more than you need in case some break coming out of tin.

CREME PATISSIERE

Mix together until pale:
2 egg yolks
2 oz ~~granulated~~ ∧ castor sugar - add
1½ oz cornflour - mix well
Bring ½ pint milk up to boil *
Pour over egg mixture.
Return to heat, keep stirring until thick -
stir in 1 tablespoon orange juice or
liqueur. Leave to get cold.

* or use ¼ pint cream + ¼ pint milk

Put a little C.P. in base of each tart. Till with the fruit (don't be mean with the fruit, pile it up). Then brush over a glaze made with some apricot preserve heated with a little lemon juice.

Almost any fruit will do - raspberries, blueberries, blackberries, strawberries are favourites.